FEATURES

The quotations on pages 7, 43, 91, 119, 149, 167, 168 and 169 are taken from Harrap's Book Of Humorous Quotations, edited by G. F. Lamb.

Cover by Susan Mayer.

Cartoons on pages 29, 75, 113, 114, 115 and 131 are extracted from Thelwell's Brat Race by Norman Thelwell. Published September 8, 1977 at £7.95 by Methuen. Copyright © Norman Thelwell.

Printed and published in Great Britain by D. C. Thomson & Co., Ltd., Dundee, Glasgow and London. © D. C. Thomson & Co., Ltd., 1992. While every reasonable care will be taken, neither D. C. Thomson & Co., Ltd., nor its agents will accept liability for loss or damage to colour transparencies or any other material submitted to this publication.

ISBN 0-85116-548-6

Price £3.60

I WAS feeling pretty low the lunchtime I landed in Juno's Snack House. It was as if I'd been cancelled out, like a mistake in a sum. In fact, that was more or less what had happened.

Even so, there must have been some self-preserving instincts at work. I was in Juno's because it was one of the places where Richard never went. For months I'd been having lunch with no-one but him, but now I was alone.

I sat on a stool at the counter — something he never liked. There was a menu card standing in front of me. I didn't really care what I had . . .

The waitress said, "Yes?"

It was too much trouble to look at the menu. She had just brought a glass of something thick and sticky for the girl on my left. "I'll have one of those," I said.

"Excuse me," the girl said

Complete Story by
PATRICIA
JOHNSTONE

to the waitress. "I wanted chocolate sauce on it, too."

The waitress took it away to be chocolate-sauced and the girl called after her, "And maybe a marshmallow or two."

I looked at the girl. She was wearing a red dress, and she was slender. You can't sit on a stool and look slender unless you really are.

"Do you often order that stuff?" I said with some respect.

"Yes," she said, not bothering to look at me. "As of this week I have it daily."

There was something grim about the way she said it.

"But isn't it terribly fattening?" I asked.

"Naturally. What do you expect from a double thick chocolate sundae?"

Well, of course. You expected flab. Suddenly it hit me that in my case it didn't matter. There was no-one to care how I looked. If I got too bulgy for my new white slacks, so what?

"Chocolate and marshmallow in mine, too, please," I said to the waitress.

The girl looked at me sideways, the way I'd been looking at her.

"You haven't been at it long," she said.

"No," I admitted. "I'm about a week late in starting."

Actually, it was one week, two days and seventeen hours since Richard had walked out of my flat for the very last time.

We ate in companionable silence for a while.

"Might as well have some pleasure in life," I said eventually.

"That's the way I see it." She sounded surprised and pleased at my intelligence.

It occurred to me we might have a lot in common.

"A man?" I asked cautiously.

"That would be flattering him."

I nodded. "A louse."

"A rotten louse," she corrected pleasantly. She took a few more gooey spoonfuls and added, "And what's more, I had to move out of my flat after his wife came to see me. You, too?"

"UNITED WE STAND!"

It was more than a motto — it was a war cry against all men! How could they know the battle was lost before it had ever begun!

5

"Yes. He ran away with my best friend," I said, and realised it was the first time I'd thought of Richard in those terms. Until then I'd wanted him back too badly.

"Honestly," I said grimly, "men are all the same. Who needs them?"

"Not me," she said determinedly, scraping up the last of her sundae. She slid off the stool.

"Nice talking to you," she said. "Maybe I'll see you here sometime."

"Hey, listen!" Suddenly I didn't want her to go. She made me feel marginally human.

"I have this empty room in my flat," I told her. "The rent's too much for me on my own. I have to find someone to share it."

"You mean that?" For a moment her face lit up.

Then she said, "No, it wouldn't work. You'd get tired of me. I told you I'm through with men and I really mean it."

"You think I don't?"

"Sooner or later you'd want to throw a romantic little candlelight dinner," she said.

"I know just who I'd want to throw it at."

Richard and I had had exactly that sort of dinner the night before I went home on holiday.

"And I do yoga in old jeans all over the floor. And I'm absolutely mad about sixteenth-century history."

"I'm a Jane Austen fanatic," I admitted. "And I've given up night cream."

"No dates at all?" she demanded.

"Believe me—from now on, if the phone ever rings it's my sister."

"You know something?" She gave a faint, out-of-practice smile. It made her look sort of brave and pretty. "I think it might just work."

"My name's Anne Briggs," I said.

"Sue Russell," she told me.

It was like the signing of a contract . . .

TWO days later Sue moved in. The flat was the end one on the fifth floor. I had left the door open to welcome her.

She shot in with a rolled-up rush mat under one arm and a pile of history books in the other.

"Quick," she panted as she dumped it all on the floor. "I've left the lift door propped open with a suitcase."

"I'll help you." I followed her back to the lift.

A man was coming towards us along the passage. He carried a large case in each hand and another tucked under his arm, and he looked as though it was no trouble at all.

"I thought you needed a hand." He beamed at us. He was big, tall and broad, with a wide, humorous mouth.

"Thank you," Sue said coldly. "We can manage."

She gave him a look which confirmed everything she'd told me about her attitude to men.

He took no notice. "You're the end flat, aren't you? I'm next door. My name's James Bartlett."

He walked straight in and put the cases on the living-room carpet. Then he stood next to them and gazed around with a pleased expression.

"Your flat looks much more lived-in than mine," he said. "I only moved in yesterday, and I haven't organised anything yet."

Sue and I stood together in silence.

"It takes time," he said cheerfully. Then he looked slightly puzzled. "Well, don't let me hold you up."

"No," Sue said.

"I expect you have a lot of things you want to do."

"Yes," I said.

"Be seeing you."

Neither of us said anything.

"I didn't know about him," I said when he'd gone. "It used to be a lady with a budgie next door."

"It's all right," Sue said kindly. "I don't suppose he'll bother us again." *Continued on page 10*

"AND I QUOTE . . ."

Jilly Cooper (1937-), British journalist and novelist, is married to publisher Leo Cooper. After working on provincial newspapers and in publishing, she became a columnist for the *Sunday Times* and *Mail on Sunday*, and has often appeared on TV. Her novels include *Prudence* (1978) and *Rivals* (1988), and her non-fiction *Men and Super Men* (1972) and *Class* (1979).

> *The most indolent women have been seen running to catch a boss.*

> *The male is a domestic animal which, if treated with firmness and kindness, can be trained to do most things.*

> *Tall girls stand about at parties looking gentle and apologetic, like Great Danes.*

> *"You worked in an office once didn't you, Jill?" a feminist once asked earnestly. "Did men ever harass you?" "Yes," I replied, "but not nearly enough."*

SEW A FINE CUSHION

This classic design will grace any room in your home — and is sure to attract compliments on your needlework.

Materials Required – Of **Anchor Tapisserie Wool:** 7 skeins Jade 0185; 3 skeins each Peach 0366, Cream 0732, Gobelin Green 0859, 0860, Moss Green 3085; and 2 skeins Peach 0835. 50 cm single thread tapestry canvas, 16 threads to 2.5 cm, 68 cm wide. 45 cm x 45 cm piece matching medium-weight fabric for backing cushion. Cushion pad to fit. Tapestry frame with 68 cm tapes. Milward International Range tapestry needle No. 18.

Mark the centre of canvas lengthwise and widthwise with a line of basting stitches. Mount canvas on frame long edges to

Key To Diagram

1 — 0860 Foundation row
2 — 0185
3 — 0859
4 — 3085
5 — 0732
6 — 0366
7 — 0835

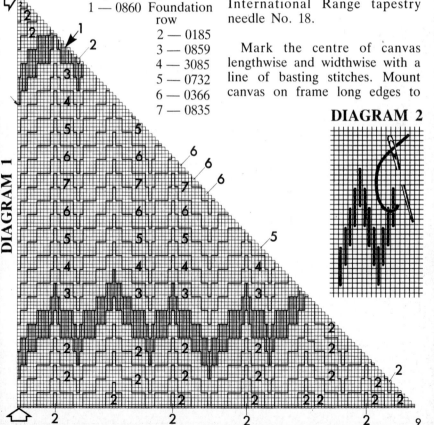

DIAGRAM 1

DIAGRAM 2

tapes. Diagram 1 gives an eighth of the design, centre indicated by blank arrows which should coincide with the basting stitches. Diagram 1 also shows the arrangement of the stitches on the threads of the canvas represented by the background lines. The design is worked throughout in Florentine Stitch. Commence the design at small black arrow 31 threads down from crossed basting stitches and work the foundation row. Work the given eighth following Diagram 1 and key to diagram. To complete one quarter repeat in reverse to the left, omitting centre stitches already worked. To complete design, turn canvas and work other three quarters in the same way. To make up, trim canvas to within 1.5 cm of embroidery on all sides. Trim backing fabric to same size, then place to embroidery, right sides together, raw edges even. Baste and stitch close to embroidery on all sides, leaving an opening on one side for pad insertion. Turn to right side, insert pad and sew open edges.

Diagram 2. Florentine Stitch. This stitch is used for working zig-zag patterns known as Florentine work. It is generally used to fill a large area and is then worked in rows of different colours forming an all-over wave pattern. The diagram shows the method of working a single row of stitches. It will be necessary to work part stitches at the diagonal and outer edges.

Continued from page 7

"I don't suppose so," I agreed, but I was feeling a little puzzled myself.

James had some highly individual quality and I couldn't think what it was. It was as though I already knew exactly what he'd be like if I ever got to know him.

But that was a backward step.

"I think he's starting to go bald already," I said cheerfully.

"I didn't notice," Sue said. She took her yoga mat and case through to her room. When she came back she said, "His mouth is as wide as an ape's."

"Yes," I agreed, but thought that maybe it wasn't quite . . .

We made sandwiches with wholewheat bread. Sue washed celery and I poured milk. We took it all through to the living-room and flopped down to eat it.

I put *Swan Lake* on the stereo. Richard used to say it was boring but it still sounded all right to me.

We ate in contented silence for a while, then Sue said, "What heavenly peace. When I think how I used to rush back from work, set my hair, take a bath, hunt desperately for something to wear, maybe even try to cook dinner . . ."

"I know. We don't bother to cook unless we feel like it now."

"It doesn't matter what we wear," she said happily. She stood up. "I'm going to finish unpacking and then I'm going to do some yoga."

When the phone rang Sue was in jeans, standing on her head.

"It'll be my sister," I said, putting my book down and going to answer it.

"Anne?" It was Richard. "Please don't hang up. I need to talk to you a minute."

My heart was beating a good deal faster than usual, I noticed with surprise. Then I remembered he was nothing in my life any more.

"There's nothing to talk about, Richard."

"Yes, there is. Jeanette and I are finished. I don't expect you to take me back, but . . ."

"I'm sorry it didn't work out for you. It's working very well for me."

"You mean . . . you've found someone already?" It was odd for him to sound so sad and humble.

"Better than that," I said smugly. "I've replaced Jeanette."

"It's no good talking on the phone," he said. "Can I come round to see you?"

"No. It really won't make any difference."

"Please let me come and explain. We can't part like this . . ."

"We already have," I interrupted. "Please don't phone again."

Sue was sitting cross-legged on the mat staring at me as I put down the receiver.

"Richard?" she said.

I nodded. I felt sorry he had been pleading.

"He's got a nerve all right," she said.

"Yes. Now he's through with Jeanette."

"It's a jungle." She shook her head slowly. "We're well out of it, Anne."

"You can say that again."

She did a few more positions and I read a page or two of my book. Then she sat up again. "What does he look like?"

"He looks all right." I wanted to be fair. "Tall, outdoor type. You see them by the dozen playing rugby on Saturdays."

She nodded and lay down on her back to relax.

WE lived in peace and harmony for more than a week. Then one afternoon I came home at five and found Sue having tea and cakes with James Bartlett.

I stared reproachfully at her and she had the grace to look embarrassed. It wasn't just any old cake, either. It was a huge, homemade one with chocolate icing and cherries.

"Come and join us." James stood up and waited until I'd sat down at the table. Funny that — I'd known all along he'd have old-fashioned manners.

I sat down and looked at Sue. She passed me a slice of cake.

"James was just telling me," she said in a rush, "that he teaches English at the High School. They had a fête today and he had to buy a cake.

Continued on page 14

KYM, Heartbreaker And Scallywag!

I GREW up with animals; we always had cats and dogs at home, and once we had guinea pigs as well — until one cold winter when they were put in the greenhouse and ate their way through my father's newly-planted and much-cherished grape vines!

After that, the guinea pigs were sold to friends who didn't have fathers who wanted grapes.

I married in wartime, and it wasn't possible to keep animals in the series of flats and furnished homes in which we began our life together. Then came our own family — a little boy, followed by a twin boy and girl. Life was far too busy for animals — almost too busy for anything in fact.

Then came the time when they all went to school and I found I had a dead house, in which nothing living moved except me.

I wanted a dog.

However, I felt that I hadn't really the time to give a dog the companionship and training that are essential if the animal is not to be a nuisance or a problem. But I went on hankering and had to content myself with taking other people's dogs for walks.

Then one day, my husband said suddenly, "What do you want most in all the world?"

Without even stopping to think, I replied, "A Siamese kitten."

He looked at me in astonishment, and said nothing more. Then six weeks later I found myself sitting in the car with a minute, bewildered

A little scrap of fur with a mind all of his own — that was Kym, says Joyce Stranger. And if he didn't like the way he was being looked after, he very quickly let us know!

and intensely miserable cream and black kitten wrapped in an old jersey.

He hated us and he hated the car. He wanted his mother and he was cold. And he didn't think much of the jersey supposed to be a substitute for his mum.

A few seconds later he discoverd a much warmer jersey — mine — and dug his way underneath, making a small, forlorn noise that we hoped was a purr.

I travelled uncomfortably, as the only place that seemed to suit him was as close to me as he could get, a habit he never grew out of if he was frightened, not even when he was old.

FROM that day on, as far as Kym was concerned, I was his mother. Whenever anything bothered him he would shin up me like an assault course. Then we would have an eye-to-eye confrontation with him on my shoulder, leaning forward and earnestly exclaiming into my face.

This performance was so uncomfortable that I learned to listen for his

12

anguished shrieks from the garden, which meant that another cat was after him, or something had alarmed him, then grab him quickly as he flew at me, and set him on my shoulder.

Once, chased by a particularly annoying beagle in the neighbourhood, he came skeltering into the kitchen as I was making pastry, and, finding that I had no hands free, swarmed up my back and sat beside my ear, declaiming for almost half an hour and obviously telling me of the horrible experience he had just been through.

Kym soon learned we were all suckers, but it was a while before we cottoned on to the fact.

There is an apple tree at the bottom of our garden, and time after time he would become marooned in this, shrieking for

Continued from page 11

"He couldn't eat it all himself so he brought it around for us to share."

She grabbed the teapot. "Have to get more water," she said and shot into the kitchen.

I began to relax. For a moment I'd actually suspected Sue of baking a cake for this man. She ought to have stopped him getting into our flat at all, but I could see that might have been difficult.

"So now you know!" James Bartlett leaned forward and smiled straight into my eyes.

Suddenly I wasn't quite as annoyed with Sue . . .

She came back and poured tea for me and refilled for herself and James. He lit a cigarette and put the match in his saucer.

Meekly Sue trotted off to find an ashtray. We hadn't needed an ashtray until now.

"I've been looking at your books, Anne," he said. "I see you like Jane Austen?"

"Yes. I think her kind of subtlety is especially appreciated by women." It was hard to be distant with him while eating his cake and being smiled at, but I was doing my best.

"Men, too," he protested. "Her sense of humour is delightful."

It had happened again. I just *knew* he'd like Jane Austen.

He didn't stay long. As soon as his cup was empty he stood up.

"Well, must be off," he said. "But I'll leave my cake for you. Don't each much cake, usually."

He smiled that smile again and left.

"I would have kept the door locked and not answered if I'd known it was him," Sue said guiltily.

"It could happen to anyone," I said soothingly. "Don't worry about it."

Considering that, she was strangely illogical about what happened on Friday.

James had knocked at our door to let us know he had bookshelves at last. Some of his books might interest me, he explained, and would I like to see them? So I went.

"But you didn't have to change into your white slacks," Sue said.

"I had to change into something! I'd just had a bath when he came and I was in my dressing-gown. Did you expect me to go like that?"

"I'm surprised you went at all. And in your navy and white tee-shirt, too."

"What's wrong with my navy and white tee-shirt?" I said crossly.

"Nothing at all — that's the whole point! You know what I'm talking about . . ."

"I just went out of politeness," I said. "I'd have done the same if it was the lady with the budgie."

"And stayed to polish off his booze?"

"I had one sherry, that's all. I don't know why you're behaving as though I'd done something sneaky."

She stared at me. "Come to think of it, I don't know either."

Suddenly she grinned and it was all over, except that I still had memories of rather a pleasant couple of hours with James Bartlett . . .

It was soon after that that Sue began buying things like wine and cigarettes. The wine was for us. We were starting to have spurts of wanting to cook exotic things. But . . . the cigarettes?

"In case we have guests," she said easily. "Neither of us smokes, but we ought to have some to offer."

"Isn't that James' brand?" I asked suspiciously.

"I don't know." She sounded surprised. "Is it?"

We didn't have many other guests. My sister and her husband came once, but it was James who was the main visitor. He popped in several times.

Once, I was in the kitchen making herb omelettes. Sue had already finished the french salad, and then he arrived.

"Hello, girls. Don't mind me. I just wondered if there was a cup of coffee on offer for a poor, hard-working man . . ."

I was the one who said, "Stay and join us, James. There's plenty of food."

That lovely smile of his lit up the whole room. "Well, thanks, Anne. I think I'll do that. Better than sardines on toast . . ."

Sue shot me a look, and I hurriedly returned to my omelettes.

Maybe it was because I was the one who'd asked him to stay that he invited me to have dinner with him.

I summoned up all my willpower and explained that Thursday evening was my pottery class night — which was perfectly true.

When I came home from pottery, the flat was empty. I prowled around for an hour or two trying to read, trying to listen to records, trying to settle on something. There was nothing worth doing.

Sue came in at eleven-thirty. She was wearing a long, rose-coloured dress. With her dark hair it looked sensational. She clicked the front door softly behind her and stood leaning against it.

"You've been out to dinner with James, haven't you?" My voice sounded hoarse.

"Yes." She smiled and drifted past me to her bedroom. She closed the door. We didn't usually bother with closing doors.

I went into my room and glared at my face in the mirror. My hair looked scraggy and very dull. But it wasn't bad enough to account for the miserable look in my eyes . . .

After a while I went and banged on Sue's door. She was sitting at the dressing-table putting cream on her face and she had her hair in shapers.

"So that's how it is," I said.

Sue shrugged. "Sorry, Anne, but that's how it is. I suppose I just don't have your strength of character. And James is so — well, so nice . . ."

"It may interest you to know something." I hadn't meant to say it,

Continued on page 18

15

rescue, which one of our three children was always delighted to do.

One day I failed to hear him, and going to look for him, found him gaily coming down the tree by himself. As soon as he saw me he froze, and clung there trying to convince me he was stuck, although he was only a foot from the ground.

We were continually learning new things about him. More than anything, for instance, he hated rain. On a wet day he would first peer daintily out of the front door at the torrents lashing down. Unconvinced, he would then storm noisily to the back door and demand that it was opened for him.

It would be raining there too, of course, and quite certain this was my fault, he would pace the hall, tail swishing, voice complaining, for half an hour, after which he would repeat the procedure. If the rain had actually deigned to stop he sat on the porch and yelled at the birds that dared trespass on *his* grass.

If it failed to stop, however, he'd stamp heavily upstairs, still shouting, to find a comfortable bed. And if it went on too long, he came to sit by me, effectively stopping me from working, while he told me how hard done by he was and how mean I was to make it rain.

KYM was a genius at producing alarms. The first time was when he "helped" my husband creosote the fence — by putting his paw in the pot and tasting it to see if it was nice.

It wasn't, of course, but before we could catch him he ran up a tree and sat there to lick the paw clean. When he finally came down in response to repeated coaxings, his mouth was in a mess as well. As creosote is poisonous, I rushed to ring the vet.

"All you can do is give him plenty of milk, bathe him to get the stuff off,

and hope," he said.

Anyone who has tried to bath a Siamese kitten covered in creosote will appreciate that the next hour was stormy in every way, with the kitten ending up wet, bedraggled, and intensely annoyed, and my arms thoroughly scratched!

Dried to a bundle of appealing fluff and given as much milk as he could conveniently drink, he settled down in my arms again and forgave me.

And very luckily, survived.

You would think he had learned sense, but not Kym.

I was writing to my sister on one of those awful days. The boiler had developed a leak, it was winter and I couldn't light the fire, the children had spots, and I had burnt the dinner.

"Nothing else can go wrong," I was just writing in the letter to my sister, when Kym walked in, stiff-legged, and crying frantically.

I couldn't imagine what was wrong. I picked him up and was shattered to discover that he was covered in varnish.

Mouth, front legs, chest, hind legs and tail, were all gummed together and set solid and shining. The vet was five miles away and my husband had the car.

Once more I rang the vet, who said the only thing to do was to cut off the fur under anaesthetic. He told me to bring him in as soon as possible as the stuff would be all over his mouth. He could have a sedative to make him sleep till morning and they would operate first thing.

I took Kym over to the vet and the next day he was duly barbered, and I went to pick him up. He was still very hazy from the anaesthetic, swearing like a trooper, and slashing at the girl who tried to pick him up, so that she refused to handle my vicious animal.

I spoke to him softly.

"Kym."

He was in my arms in an instant, trying to get under my clothing. I put on his collar and lead and held him in my arms, to cross the road to the car park — and I just missed death.

A swerving lorry driver was unable to take his eyes off a demented woman holding a Siamese cat that was not merely wearing a collar and lead like a dog, but had furthermore been clipped like a poodle. And although the vet had tidied him, as far as possible, he had a number of bald patches, including all of his tail except for three inches of black fur at the end.

He looked distinctly odd for months, in fact.

ABOUT this time Kym matured and decided that all the gardens in the road belong to him, regardless of whether other cats lived there.

On one occasion I tried to stop a fight. Stupidly, I put my hand on Kym as he was running away. Had I spoken, all would have been well.

Kym thought he was being attacked by another cat from the rear and turned and raked my bare arms with his hind claws, which were pretty powerful at the end of those driving hind legs.

As soon as he realised it was me, he was appalled, and came up into my arms, purring and rolling, frantically saying he hadn't meant it, not at all.

Both of us had injections that time.

Then, when he was about three, Kym developed cat flu and was desperately ill for two weeks.

For 10 days he lay still in his bed, his only food glucose and water. We were beginning to give up and the vet gave us a deadline:

"If he's no better by Thursday, he's suffering too much . . ."

We walked around as if we too were under sentence of death. By the Wednesday evening, Kym was no better, and my husband had a look at him.

"We can't do him much further harm," he said. "Suppose we try a little brandy?"

We gave him half a teaspoonful from a medicine dropper. It would have been better if it had been diluted and given gradually but we didn't know that then. The brandy went down, and for the first time for two weeks, Kym responded by moving his head, trying to avoid the taste.

A few minutes later, very groggily, he sat up and tried to wash his paw. I sat beside him and he started to scramble on to my lap. Lifted into a haven he had not sampled for two weeks, he managed a very out-of-practice, rusty purr.

By morning, Kym was able to eat a little bone broth, and when the vet arrived, expecting to have to put him down, he was greeted by a purr, and went away delighted that his visit had ended so well.

BY that time we owned a touring caravan and spent all our holidays taking off into the wildest places we could find in England, Scotland and Wales, where we could watch ospreys fishing, and foxes slipping quietly downhill at dawn.

Kym came too, hating the car when it cornered or braked, and constantly shouting as vehicles approached us.

It was in Scotland, near Fort William, that Kym had his worst adventure. We had left him in the caravan, and shut all the windows as we were parked beside a very busy main road.

It seemed that Prince Philip was taking Prince Charles and Princess Anne along the Crinan Canal in a boat. He was due to pass through Fort William that day, and the passing cars on the road never stopped.

Continued overleaf.

Continued from previous page.

We needed to go to the bank before going on with our tour and we rather wished the Royal Family had consulted us so that our holiday dates didn't clash!

It took far longer than we expected to go to the bank. We got back, opened the caravan door, and found it empty.

A tiny ventilator was pushed as far open as it would go.

No Kym.

We searched the field calling, until I heard an agonised yowl from a large clump of bracken. I ran over and Kym came out of the bracken.

He was covered in blood, and his right hind leg dragged behind him, with two splinters of bone sticking through the fur on his thigh.

I lifted him gently.

I have often wondered if anyone ever told the Royal children of the extraordinary cortège that walked through the centre of Fort William the afternoon that they passed through.

I wore a bloodstained dress, and carried a large rectangular tray, on which was a pad of newspaper and an inert and faintly wailing Siamese cat, covered by a wad of paper tissues.

Behind me, at a distance, came my husband and sons, all with set and sombre faces, and behind them, wailing at the top of her voice, came our daughter, who was then only 10 years old.

At last we found the vet's house tucked away up a side road. He could do very little, as he was a large-animal vet, used to cattle. He could deal with ordinary cat and dog

Continued on page 21

Continued from page 15

but suddenly I couldn't stop myself. "It so happens James invited *me* to have dinner first."

"I know," she said. "Did you think he'd try to hide it?"

Somehow that hurt. It hurt that she knew as much about him as I did, and possibly more.

"How long is it," I said slowly, "since you had a chocolate sundae?"

"I don't remember," she said lightly. "To be honest, I find them a bit sickly."

"Me, too." I turned to go. "And don't be too sure of my strength of character."

I could have said more, but the rest was too private. It was too simple, too much a cliché, too much the thing people said when they didn't even know what it meant.

I was in love with James. I knew exactly what it meant. It meant pain and longing and uncertainty, and terrible hope.

A dozen red rosebuds were delivered to me at the flat the next day. My heart leapt to the sky until I read the card. *Just to prove we're still friends, Richard.*

That was the trouble with hope . . .

Sue rescued the roses and put them in water. She read the card, too. "Why don't you let him come and see you? Anyone can make a mistake, and he's trying to make up for it."

"I appreciate your advice on a lot of things," I said. "This isn't one of them."

O N Saturday morning we finally realised how bad things had become. And no-one was even bothering to hide the fact that it was because of James.

I spent two hours hunting for a really beautiful dress. And I found it — a very plain one in brown and gold, with only the perfect fit to hint at how much it had cost. I wore it home because it felt so good.

Sue was in the living-room doing her nails when I arrived. She had on a new yellow trouser suit and a creamy shirt. Her hair had been cut short as a boy's by someone fiendishly clever with scissors. Her make-up looked marvellous.

We stared at each other.

"Wow! What did it cost you?" she asked me, wide-eyed.

I told her.

"It was worth every penny," was her only comment.

"And you?"

She told me. "I had a facial as well, you see."

I nodded. "You didn't waste your money either."

We sat in silence for a while. She filed another nail.

Eventually I said, "We can't go on like this, Sue. I'll be broke until the end of next month."

"Me, too." Sue stared into space and looked thoughtful. "James must decide," she said.

She took a deep breath. "We'll each give a romantic little dinner for two. We'll have James round one at a time, right?"

We tossed a coin over who would be first. I lost.

"I'll ask him if he can come tonight," Sue said. "We're all right for food. Could you arrange to be out?"

"I'll go to my sister," I said. "She'll be overjoyed if I offer to babysit."

Suddenly I knew I couldn't spend the afternoon in the flat while she organised the dinner. "I'll go soon and be out of your way."

"That's very sporting of you," Sue said.

I didn't feel sporting. When I thought about her and James together I had some primitive, savage feelings that surprised even me.

I managed to get through the evening. Having to babysit made it easier. After all, you can't lie down and die with a nine-month-old niece grinning at you from her cot and wanting to play.

My sister and brother-in-law jumped at the chance to go to a late show, and it was after midnight when he dropped me off at the flat. That would be late enough, I thought to myself.

I was torn between hoping the dinner had been a flop and James had gone home early, and that he would still be waiting there to see me.

When I got in, the living-room was empty. Sue had gone to bed.

One glance at the table told me her dinner had been a riotous success. There was an empty wine bottle. The candles had burnt low.

Richard's red roses, which might have started off as a centrepiece, had been placed on the floor against the wall.

Sue was asleep. There was nothing left for me to do but go to bed.

I couldn't bear to think about Sue's dinner-party, so I lay in bed thinking about mine. It was going to be the most beautiful, romantic thing that had ever happened to James . . .

SUE slept late that Sunday morning and eventually emerged from her room, sleepy and glowing.

"Coffee?" she said.

"How was your dinner?" I asked as casually as possible.

She sighed and hugged herself. "What a marvellous man."

"You've still got one earring on," I said coldly.

"Have I?" She smiled at me fondly. "I was going to fetch something. What was it?"

Grimly I handed her a cup of coffee.

She sat in a chair, took one sip and put the cup down. She flopped back and smiled at the ceiling.

"So James enjoyed the dinner?"

"James?" She went on smiling for a while. Then she sat up straight and said, "How do you mean, James?"

"James Bartlett — he lives next door. Remember?"

"Oh, him. He went home early. He said he had flu coming on, and couldn't eat a thing. Naturally, I was talking about Richard."

Richard? I couldn't see what was natural about that at all . . .

"He came to see you just after you left, and he stayed for dinner. Anne, why didn't you tell me? He's so . . . so *wonderful!*"

"James has flu," I said indignantly, "and you didn't even bother to mention it! He could be desperately ill, all alone in his flat, and you'd just leave him to battle it out . . ."

"He didn't look very bad," Sue said.

I was already in the kitchen, mixing honey and lemon juice.

"Listen," Sue shouted through, "why don't you change into your white slacks and that tee-shirt?"

But I was already on my way out of the flat.

James let me in as soon as I knocked. He didn't look ill, exactly. He looked as though he'd been under a strain. He'd been reading the Sunday papers and his ashtray was full of cigarette ends.

We sat down opposite each other. He smiled straight into my eyes and I couldn't think of anything to say. It was like trying to drive west in the late afternoon.

I looked down at the glass of amber liquid in my hand. I couldn't remember what it was.

He said, "Hello, Anne."

It was several minutes late for him to be saying that.

I looked up. "Hello."

And then I saw we were starting to recognise each other . . .

——————— * **THE END** * ———————

20

Continued from page 18

emergencies, but we realised that Kym's was a far from ordinary case.

He gave Kym an injection, and told us we would give the cat a better chance if we took him to the Royal Veterinary College in Glasgow — a piece of advice that proved to have long-reaching results.

We were given a small, deep-sided cardboard box and told to keep him in that, preventing him from moving if possible. He also told us to call back in the morning for another injection before travelling the long road to Glasgow.

We spent the night drinking cups of tea and were up by six. We left for Glasgow with a tranquillised cat, on the wettest day I have ever seen in my life, even in Scotland.

Tranquillised?

Kym reacted to the tranquilliser by going berserk. I fought him, enduring bites and scratches, determined to keep him still. Finally I put him in the box and put the box on the seat beside me so that I could hold him down. He systematically tore the box all the way to Glasgow.

We found the Royal College at last. The vets were marvellous, reassuring and hopeful. The leg was X-rayed and proved to have been broken at the ball joint of the hip. There was nothing they could do except immobilise him in a small cage.

There was still a week of our holiday left and they told us that by the time we were ready to go home he should be fit to travel. With luck, they added, he would only be left with a slight limp. But meanwhile there was a risk that he would die of shock.

We had no idea what had happened to Kym, but the vet suggested he had been run over by a car.

We left him and went away to a silent van, and gloom. We rang the College every day, and on the third day were told that Kym wouldn't eat, and there was very little hope. I was about to ring off when I thought to ask what they were feeding him on.

It was a famous proprietary cat food, and I knew that even in the best of health, Kym would rather starve than eat it. When I told them this, the veterinary assistant asked me what his favourite food was.

Kym loved fish but as it was a Sunday, there was little hope of them finding any, I knew. But a cheerful voice said that that gave them a chance and asked me to ring again the next day.

When I rang the following morning, I was told that one of the girls had gone down to the docks for fresh fish as the boats came in; Kym had eaten well and was eating now, and there was all the hope in the world!

We were very sold on Glasgow — so much so, that years later our younger son decided he would be a vet and would like to train at Glasgow. He did, and is now married to a vet and working in a busy, small animal practice in London.

WE went to pick Kym up on the way home, on a fine sunny day. I watched a horse being taken across the yard, limping, while two vets examined him. He looked like a racehorse, a lovely animal, but my mind was only half on him. I was waiting for my cat, expecting a feeble invalid.

The horse stopped close to me. I can never resist any animal and they all know it. Dogs always rush up to me, and cats come to be picked up. Most horses seem to know I like them, and this was no exception. I patted him and spoke.

He turned his head in amazement, as from behind me came the loudest Siamese yell I have ever heard in my life.

Kym had heard my voice, and the

girl holding him was reduced to laughter as she hurried over to me.

Conversation was impossible, he went on and on and on, telling me everything that had happened to him in the past week, chiding me for leaving him there, melting up to me, purring and talking all in one breath. He never stopped all the way home.

At first he could not walk at all, but kept falling over. Then he began to walk on three legs, and just for a second, put his weight on his fourth leg. A few days later he took a few steps and collapsed.

Gradually he built up the strength in that leg, stubbornly determined, never giving up.

Within a month he was going upstairs, not like a cat but like a rabbit, with both hind legs together, thump, thump, thump. He weighed a ton, so this was a very noisy operation.

He would not let me out of sight, and it was on the first time we went into the garden together I knew he *had* been run over. We were quite safe in the garden, but near the fence, and as a car turned into the road he screamed and lumbered towards me. Being unable to jump, he clawed up at me to get into my arms, where he lay, every muscle rigid, ears flat.

As a result of the accident, Kym became left-pawed instead of right-pawed, as he fell over if he used his right paw, which was in front of the injured leg.

He could never open the door properly while he was disabled, and he solved this by lying down by the door, hooking his left paw round it, and then inching forward to get his head in and open the door more fully. Then he stood up and limped out.

Within six months, he was climbing trees again and running as swiftly as ever; back to battling with his enemies; and no-one would guess that one leg was shorter than the other, as he learned to sidle swiftly in a very odd snaking movement, and he enjoyed life immensely, in spite of his leg.

But cats grow old, and in time Kym slowed down — though he never admitted to age, and he never gave up rushing to me when things annoyed him.

And, even when Kym was 12, he still played his "goodnight game," one that was very annoying when I was tired and it was late.

As soon as he realised we were preparing for bed, he bolted upstairs and raced round the house in a mad game of hide and seek, trying to avoid being put in his bed downstairs. He would look up with a melting expression when I caught him, purring, obviously asking not to be put away by himself, not tonight, just this once . . .

WHEN I was on my own and my family and husband away, Kym did come and sleep at the bottom of my bed towards the end of his days.

The family by then were all grown-up and my husband had gone on a business trip. I went to bed, and in the night heard the thump of glass, five times. I switched on the light and saw the cat sitting up, ears pricked, looking downstairs.

Burglars!

I have a phone extension by my bed, and I picked it up, dialling 999. I got through and there was one more crash. I explained the position.

"Lock your bedroom door," a reassuring voice said. "We'll be there in five minutes."

I locked the door.

It was the longest five minutes I have ever spent. It was 3.15 a.m. and all the houses around me were dark.

The doorbell rang.

I tried to unlock the door. It had never been locked before, and the lock had jammed. By the time I did get the door open any intruder would have fled, as one policeman was still ringing the doorbell and the other was calling up to my lighted bedroom window to ask if I were OK.

I was. Just.

Kym by now was thoroughly scared, and I often wonder what the police thought when the front door was opened by a woman in a Father-Christmas-red dressing-gown wearing an annoyed Siamese cat like a scarf round her neck. Kym proceeded to tell both men how alarmed we were as they searched the house.

Nothing.

No-one.

They went, and in the morning I found six oranges that had rolled out of a bowl on to a glass table. Feeling an idiot, I rang the police.

"Rather a false alarm than have something wrong," they said. "And it must have sounded very frightening in the night. Don't worry. And call us next time as we'd rather come than fail to come when something is really wrong."

KYM was 13 before he showed signs of illness. He grew slow and spent most of his time lying in the shrubs in the garden, under the winter jasmine, or the veronica bush, asleep in the sun. Always ready to greet us or to purr when picked up, but not always ready to eat, though by now he was so fat the vet was sure I was overfeeding him.

He became very ill when we were away, and my daughter was looking after him. I came home to find a cat that could barely move. I rang the vet, who said, "Well?" He had seen him that day. I just said, "Yes, but at home, please."

The vet was coming at ten. I lifted Kym, and he startled me by rolling and purring, rubbing himself against my hand in ecstasy of affection that I had never seen before. He went on and on, and then, quite suddenly, he lay limp and exhausted.

I was very glad when the vet came.

We had a post-mortem. Kym had had cancer. Luckily it had only just begun to trouble him.

The day he died I went into the garden, and saw him under a bush. I was startled, sure I was seeing ghosts, but when I looked, the black cat next door had appropriated Kym's favourite place in the sun. I turned to come in and discovered there was a ginger cat under the winter jasmine.

That day was unnerving. At one time there were eight cats in my garden, and they came back and back again, as if they knew there was no cat to challenge them.

They didn't go until I bought my pup.

It's a long time now since Kym died, but he was such a character that he remains in memory. Animals come; and they go after too short a time, but to me, each one is a preparation for the next; the future is there, to look forward to, to sharing a different part of life with a different sort of animal. No two are alike.

Out of all the cats I have had, Kym will remain the greatest character. Not the favourite; all of them are that.

I hope the world never becomes so sophisticated that animals are outlawed. Those of us who live with them and need them prefer a simpler life; work at a gentler pace; and know that man is not all-important, as we are providers of comfort, moppers-up of wet dogs — born, those animals know, for only one thing, and that is provide for them, be we queens or commoners. ∎

The Book "Kym" by Joyce Stranger is published by Michael Joseph.

ONLY five minutes to go before she could shut up the shop for a whole hour of pure, uninterrupted peace, Laura Benson thought thankfully. Never had the hands moved so slowly round the clock as they had this Friday morning.

Since eight o'clock, when she'd opened the doors of the small sweet shop she managed during the week, she had longed for lunchtime — and a chance to think. To try, once more, to sort out her thoughts and plan exactly what she would say to Adam when she saw him on Saturday.

Automatically she served the seemingly endless stream of children as they thrust their money forward for penny chews, liquorice laces and sherbet dabs till at last the five minutes were over and she could lock up.

Laura leaned for a moment against the old-fashioned door, its jangling bell temporarily silent, and felt suddenly very tired and far older than her 28 years.

She made her way up the steep, narrow staircase at the back of the shop with its boxes of sweets stacked either side of it, and heaved a sigh of relief. Then she slipped off her shoes and sank into the big old armchair with a long-awaited cup of coffee.

She glanced around the little flat she shared with Cindy, her six-year-old daughter. It was tiny — hardly more than a cupboard, her mother had called it — when she had been trying to persuade Laura to move in with them after Steve had died so suddenly.

But it was home, and she loved it.

Yes, Steve had gone, and the flat was the one concrete piece of evidence, besides Cindy, that she had of her life with him.

It was all so much a part of him — the books lining the shelves, the sailing trophies . . .

"The second love of my life, darling," he'd told her more than once. But Laura knew deep down, that however much he had loved her and Cindy, it was sailing that had been the real passion in his life.

To have taken that away would have been like depriving him of the breath of life; but it was bitterly ironic that it had been his love of the water that had been his end. Steve, with his vibrant energy for living, had died, leaving her with an enchanting daughter blessed with her father's laughing blue eyes.

It hadn't been easy managing without him. Laura had begun by taking Cindy to her mother's on the other side of the town each morning before opening the shop, and fetching her back in the evening, but it had been too much for a child of four years old, so she'd had to stop it.

Laura's parents had tried to reason with her.

"Why not move in with us, dear?" her mother had pleaded. "You can have your own bed-sitting room, we don't have to be under each other's feet."

Complete Story by JANET HARTSHORNE

24

LEAVE IT TO CINDY

She had made up her mind she'd found just the daddy she was looking for. All she had to do now was convince her mother . . .

"You could find yourself a better job," her father had added. "One you really enjoy. After all, you only manage that poky little shop because the flat goes with it."

Laura had known they were right but she knew also she could never bring herself to leave all that she and Steve had built up together.

So she decided to leave Cindy with her parents during the week and collect her on Friday evenings to spend the weekend with her.

It had been lonely at first, but gradually Laura had grown accustomed to her own company, even preferring it at times. Several times she had been asked out but she'd always refused. It seemed somehow disloyal to Steve not to.

Besides, no-one could even hold a candle to him, she often told herself. And there were always the weekends and Cindy to look forward to . . .

Laura would always try to arrange something special for the two of them to do; a trip to the zoo, a picnic in the park or a visit to the cinema.

But while it was obvious Cindy loved it all, it seemed to be the ritualistic, routine things which pleased her most, lying tucked up in bed, while Laura read to her, the visit downstairs to buy her sweets from old Mrs Ferguson who managed the shop on Saturdays, the inevitable games of Snap and Snakes and Ladders — and more recently, Adam's visits.

IT had been through Cindy that Laura had met Adam Hunt. They had been feeding the ducks at the lake in the park and when all the bread was finished, Cindy had wandered off on her own to explore.

Laura had been content to sit by the lake, and it was some time before she had realised that Cindy was nowhere to be seen.

For 10 minutes she had called and searched frantically, not daring to move far from the seat in case Cindy came back.

Never had she been as relieved as when she saw the tall young man appear, leading a subdued Cindy by the hand, her face dirty and tear-streaked but nonetheless doing justice to a huge ice-cream cornet.

"It's all right, Mummy," Cindy had reassured her.

"This man found me. He bought me this ice-cream . . . and his name's Adam," she'd added, gazing adoringly up at the man by her side.

"Thank you so much, I was nearly frantic," she had told Adam, as she'd tried to clean up the little girl's face.

"An ice-cream was obviously the thing to cheer your daughter up, but I think you could do with something stronger," he'd said. "How about a cup of coffee?"

And she'd let herself be led to the small café nearby, where he'd ordered a milk shake for Cindy and coffee for Laura and himself.

Laura had never really had time to think whether she was being disloyal to Steve's memory. And besides, he was so different . . .

He was tall and rather too thin with a gentle, compassionate face, and the glasses he wore sometimes gave him a deceptive, serious look.

No, there had been no chance to think twice about Adam; he had been there when she'd needed him — and ever since, it seemed.

And now, after eight months of Laura, Cindy and Adam, he suddenly made his ultimatum that meant it would soon be just Laura and Cindy again . . .

She had become so secure in the warmth of his company that she'd never thought about it ending.

It had been such an uncomplicated, comfortable relationship. Often he would arrive at the flat unexpectedly and they would sit for hours listening to records, talking, or sometimes just sitting, happy in each other's company. She had been completely unaware of the change taking place until it was too late.

THEY had just returned from driving Cindy back to her parents' home one weekend, when Laura had realised that something was missing from the easy atmosphere which usually existed between them. But even then, she hadn't been prepared for what followed.

"Laura, how do you really feel about me?" he had asked her suddenly, and her heart had thumped madly at his step into unfamiliar territory.

"I like you very much, Adam. You must know that," she'd told him uncertainly. "You — you're the dearest friend I've ever had."

"And that's all?" he'd replied quietly and smiled. "I don't know how to say this, but if it is, I'm afraid it isn't enough any more. Don't you see, Laura? It might have been once but I wasn't in love with you then."

She'd felt a mixture of surprise and — almost panic.

"And now you think you are?" she'd asked, and Adam had nodded.

"Now, I *know* I am, Laura. I want to marry you —"

"No!" she'd cried. "I'm sorry, Adam, but no, I — I'm fond of you, very fond of you, but — I'm not in love with you. I can't be. I know I won't . . ."

"What you mean is you won't *let* yourself be, because you feel that would be betraying Steve, don't you?" he'd probed gently. "But Steve belongs to the past, Laura, he should just be a beautiful memory to cherish now, not your reason for living."

She'd said nothing, and Adam had gone on:

"If you can only remember him and be sad then it's far better to forget and be happy, because nothing can bring him back and no-one can live with a memory for ever. Not and survive."

"You're saying it's possible to forget to order," she'd protested angrily. "But believe me it isn't."

Adam had shaken his head.

"No, I'm not saying that, but it *is* possible to remember to order and I think that's what you're doing."

It was then, before she could say anything, that he had broken the news that he would be leaving shortly to take up a job in Canada.

"I want to marry you, Laura," he'd told her. "So please think about it. But if you know in your heart you'll never really love me, then don't marry me for any other reason. Much as I love you and want to look after you and Cindy, I need you to love me, too."

He had gone on to point out that they would be able to come back every year so that her parents wouldn't be losing Cindy altogether, and Laura had thought how considerate it was of Adam to think of others, even in the midst of his own problems.

If she could ever love anyone again, she knew it would be Adam. The thought of him going away was unbearable and she realised how much she had come to depend on him during the last few months.

But she knew, too, that she could never marry him. To do that she would have to leave the flat, and all the memories it contained of her happy life with Steve, and that she could never do — not even for Adam . . .

L AURA looked around her now, remembering how she and Steve had trailed around second-hand shops during the early days, picking up bits and pieces for the flat. the big, comfortable armchair, the old coach lantern hanging in the corner, and the little jugs and ornaments that were still on the shelves . . .

She turned to take a last look round the room before making her way back down to the shop, imagining again the hours spent there with Steve. His old rocking-chair still stood in its original place by the bookshelves, but it was with confused emotions that she realised that, try as she might to do otherwise, it was not the carefully-preserved picture of Steve that flitted across her mind, but Adam's . . .

And tomorrow, on Cindy's seventh birthday, he would be back from the business trip that had taken him away for a week, and sooner or later she would have to give him her final answer . . .

But first she was determined that they should all enjoy Cindy's birthday. Later, when the little girl was in bed, she would tell Adam she couldn't marry him, could never give up all she had had with Steve and put him behind her. Not even for a lifetime of happiness.

★   ★   ★   ★

Cindy was awake earlier than usual the following morning in spite of a late night, and anxious to open her presents.

Laura had bought her a quilted dressing-gown in palest blue just like her own, with slippers to match. Cindy had flung her arms round Laura's neck in delight.

"Oh, Mummy, it's the loveliest present I ever had. Now I'll be just like you. Tonight when I've had my bath, I'll put them on so that Adam can see me in them."

Laura smiled down at her daughter, trying not to think of other birthdays when there would be no Adam there . . .

thelwell's BRAT RACE
THE LITTLE STRANGER

To most parents the birth of a child is an event that calls for celebration.

Few fathers find their offspring very attractive at first.

Babies have a surprisingly strong grip — which they find difficult to release.

Experts recommend getting them into a playgroup as soon as possible.

The parcel that had arrived from Steve's parents contained a soft, cuddly rabbit to hold her nightdress, and it was immediately given pride of place at the head of her bed.

Lastly came Laura's own parents' present, a tiny, silver, heart-shaped locket that opened to reveal spaces for photographs.

"Ooh, Mummy," Cindy whispered. "Isn't it beautiful?"

And even before she was dressed, the sitting-room floor was covered with an assortment of small photographs as she searched for two suitable ones to put in it.

L AURA was making breakfast for the two of them when she was suddenly aware of Cindy standing in the doorway watching her, clutching several photographs in her hand.

"Why so serious, darling?" she asked, when she saw the expression on her daughter's face. "Having trouble deciding which ones to use?"

Cindy nodded, and Laura smiled.

"Never mind, I'll be through in a minute and we'll look together."

Cindy kept the photographs, face downwards, beside her while they ate their breakfast. She was unusually quiet, and Laura knew far more was going on in her daughter's mind than she could fathom at the moment.

"Right, now," she said, clearing a space before them on the table, "let's decide about these pictures, shall we?" *Continued on page 33*

YOU'VE seen him at the cinema many times . . . the small boy with freckles and a sheepish expression cradling some small appealing creature. "Let me keep him," he begs. His mother finally relents and the animal is allowed to stay with the family.

It's certainly a very familiar scene in our house, with one exception — it's my husband who always plays the main part!

We started in a small way with a Labrador dog. I'd seen the signs and rushed out to buy him before my husband beat me to it with a Great Dane or an Irish Wolfhound.

Then came the "Age of Wire Netting," brought about by my husband's desire for feathered

---

by DENISE HAWTHORNE

At first I quite liked the idea of having a few pets about the house, says Denise Hawthorne. But now all those dogs, chickens, rabbits and finches really are getting my goat!

We Live A Very Wild

friends. There was frantic hammering and sawing and children carrying nails . . . it went on for months. I didn't worry because I never really expected the roosts to be finished. I should have known better.

The budgies and finches *are* very pretty to watch from the kitchen window, and the babies have a certain appeal, squeaking away in the nest boxes.

However, I made it clear that the housekeeping could not support another 20 beaks, so every spring I bore my friends rigid with the delights of these small feathered things, begging them to have one.

Later, chickens seemed a good idea.

"Think of the money we'd save on eggs," I was told. "And when they've finished laying we can always put them in the pot."

There was more wire netting and weekend hammerings resulting in the most incredible hen house you've ever seen.

Shall I just say that it started life as a dining-room table, and the rest of it is composed entirely of assorted pieces of wood that just happened to be lying about the garden doing nobody any harm.

The hens might have layed sooner if the dog hadn't harassed them. For weeks all they seemed to do was moult and eat. I eventually stood amongst them and delivered a heartfelt speech about the exorbitant price of hen food, and how I'd got a good-sized roasting tin that could accommodate the best of them.

It must have worked, for the very next day we got an egg. The chicken wanted to eat it, but as it had cost me approximately six pounds, I wanted it preserved, for all time!

Eventually all the hens got the message, and soon we were having more omelettes and soufflés than we would have chosen. I fully expected to start crowing.

ACTUALLY, I'm quite fond of the rabbits, useless though they are.

These delightful creatures are named Freeman, Hardy and Willis, and in the true free-range tradition they secretly and laboriously plan escape bids . . .

We've wasted many a weekend chasing them and blocking up holes, only to discover that they always returned home after dark anyway.

At this point, my husband decided the dog was left out, as he hadn't anything of his own size to play with — and that's when he came home with a goat.

It was a gentle, affectionate creature guaranteed to put the lawn mower out of business. He cried for his mother for the first few nights, scaring the neighbours.

However, he's settled down very nicely now, except he thinks he's a Labrador, too, and can't understand why he's not allowed beyond the back door.

As you can imagine, this mini-zoo we've built up presented a bit of a problem when holidays came

Continued overleaf.

▲ Lucky actually belongs to a neighbour, but spends many happy hours with Mrs B. Brown of Llangollen.

◄ Mrs J. Fairclough of St Helens reveals that Marco, her pet King Charles Cavalier Spaniel, gained fame locally in a TV programme called "On The Waterfront."

Continued from previous page.

round. My in-laws consented to take over, and I gave the animals all a good talking-to before we left.

While we were away, the hens actually laid their eggs in the right places, and the goat and the dog played together in the long grass.

It was the rabbits that let us down. They had become quite wild by this time, and more adventurous, and there were several phone calls about missing sprouts and desecrated lettuce beds.

My father-in-law made a desperate midnight bid to barricade them in while they were asleep, but they must have been having a night on the town, because they came home haggard and tired the morning after.

He sat out one night with a great blanket to catch them up in, but all that resulted in was a wild story rapidly spreading through the village about a cloaked figure being seen prowling the street at two in the morning.

We did catch them eventually, however, and they are now confined in a more substantial pen and subjected to daily inspections for tunnels.

I wouldn't have minded all this quite so much if my husband had been a deprived child, forbidden so much as a tiny white mouse, but he had all the usual pets when he was young.

Nowadays, as I struggle into my wellies and set off down the garden with assorted containers full of food, I plan my revenge.

There's a small field we haven't filled yet. That would do nicely for a pet all of my very own. They say alligators make good watchdogs, and they're so cute when they're little . . . ■

32

MEET A *PET*

▲ Sam, in Hebden Bridge, doesn't mind Kaomi, Mrs J. Priestley's granddaughter, pretending he's a pony.

◀ Toby and Oliver, three-year-old brothers, have met the TV vet, James Herriot, Mrs P. Cox of Bath tells us.

Continued from page 29

"I want to put that one in." Cindy thrust forward a photograph of Laura taken on a trip to the coast last summer. "And then I want to . . ."

She hesitated, her blue eyes warily surveying Laura's face.

"Yes, Cindy?"

"I want to put that in the other side."

She was holding out a picture of Adam, taken in the park with Cindy as they had shared a private joke.

Cindy was still watching her intently, waiting for some sign that she approved, or . . . what else was a child of seven capable of discerning, Laura wondered uneasily.

She struggled not to show any sign of surprise at the choice. She had been sure the other photograph would be of Steve. Oh, she realised that Cindy's memory of her father must be hazy, she had been only four years old when he had died. But Laura had tried to keep what memories she had of him alive.

Cindy was putting the remaining photograph back with the other discarded ones now, and, glancing down, Laura saw that it was one of Steve taken years before Cindy had been born. A young, immature boy Cindy could never have known.

She looked down at the photograph of Adam and Cindy.

"I think it's a wonderful idea," she made herself say. "Adam will think so, too. Come on, I'll cut them out for you."

The little girl's face was beaming as they fitted the tiny portions of

C

the photographs into the locket and placed it round her neck. Turning, she wrapped her soft arms round Laura and hugged her.

"I've put the two people I love most of all in the whole world in my locket, Mummy."

And then, anxiously:

"Granny and Grandpa won't be hurt, will they?"

"Oh, darling, of course they won't. They'll think it's a lovely idea, too," Laura assured her as she knelt and began clearing up the scattered photographs.

"Mummy." The childish voice sounded oddly uncertain.

"I was going to put Daddy in my locket." She hesitated for a moment, and Laura couldn't bring herself to look up as she saw Steve's face smiling up at her from the pile of rejected photographs.

"You don't mind me not putting Daddy in, do you?"

Laura took the little girl into her arms.

"Cindy, of course I don't mind. It's your present and you must decide who to put in it."

Kneeling there on the floor, their eyes were level and Cindy gazed unwaveringly into Laura's. She sighed quietly.

"You see, Mummy, I sort of love Daddy, too, but . . ."

A small frown puckered her brow as she strove to find the right words. "He's like a dream . . . something you remember but isn't there any more. I love Adam such a lot and he is . . . well, Adam is a *now* person."

"Yes, Cindy," she whispered. "Adam is a now person."

A N excited Cindy announced Adam's arrival, just as Laura was putting the finishing touches to the birthday tea.

"Well, and how are my two favourite girlfriends?" he asked above Cindy's shrieks.

"Adam, Adam, look at my locket and guess who's in it!" Cindy insisted, tugging at his coat. "It's the two people I love best in the whole world."

"Donald Duck and Mickey Mouse?" he said.

"No! Silly." Cindy giggled. "It's you and Mummy. Look!"

Adam stooped down to the little girl's height, and his eyes met Laura's over the curly head before he bent and planted a kiss on it.

"That, Cindy, is the nicest thing anyone has ever done for me. Thank you," he told her shakily. "And now, somewhere, I should have a present for you, too."

He drew a small package from his pocket and handed it to her.

"Ooh, Adam, it's lovely!" Cindy exclaimed, as she unwrapped the charm bracelet.

"What do the charms mean?"

"Well, first of all there's the aeroplane," Adam began. "Like the one which will be taking me to Canada soon."

"Honestly, Adam? Can I come with you?"

Laura caught her breath as Adam looked up and raised an inquisitive brow, but she said nothing.

"That will depend, Cindy," Adam went on, and pointed again to the bracelet. "Now this little fella here is a duck. Because the first time I saw you was when you had been feeding the ducks."

"And you found me when I was crying." Cindy laughed.

"Yes, I found you. And the last one is a heart to show you that I love you just as much as you love me. There are only three charms yet but each birthday I'll buy you another till you have lots," he promised her.

"Oh, Adam," she told him, hugging him. "I'm glad it was you who found me."

"So am I, darling. So am I."

Quietly, Laura turned and went into the kitchen. Adam followed her, closing the door behind him before turning her round to face him.

"After a week of absolute agony, I don't intend waiting one moment longer," he said firmly. "So at the risk of spoiling the rest of Cindy's birthday, tell me. Do you love me enough to marry me now?"

"Can I ask you one or two questions first?" she asked him evasively.

"All right, fire away!"

"Does missing you every minute you were away mean I love you?" He smiled. "Could do."

"And being incredibly disappointed every time the telephone rings and it isn't your voice at the other end?"

"More than likely," he murmured, drawing her closer.

"Wanting to spend every day of the rest of my life with you . . . ?"

"Without a shadow of doubt."

"Then I think I must love you very much indeed."

"That's all I wanted to know," he said, kissing her. "Now I'll give Cindy her other present."

They went back into the sitting-room where Adam told Cindy to close her eyes.

"Quick!" the little girl squealed as she stood, eyes screwed tight shut and hands outstretched. "My eyes will open themselves in a minute. I know they will."

"You can look now." Adam laughed as he laid the thin piece of card on the small palms.

"It's a ticket," Cindy breathed. "To Canada!"

"Right first time."

"For — for me?"

"Yes, Cindy. For you," he said with a smile.

Cindy turned, bewildered, to Laura.

"Are we going on a holiday, Mummy?" she asked. "You and me and Adam?"

Laura looked up at Adam as he slipped an arm round her.

"Yes, Cindy. You and me and Adam."

—————— * **THE END** * ——————

ASK anyone for the name of a cookery book author and it's almost certain that they'll reply, "Mrs Beeton."

Yet this lady, famous as she has become, is only one of many who down the years have written books on the culinary arts.

Looking back to the days when meals consisted of scores of dishes, and when it took several hours to eat them, it's fairly obvious that a cook's manual would have been a necessity in every large kitchen. Yet, the earliest known work is one by the Chief Cook to Richard II.

This overworked individual had to prepare — in addition to unspecified loads of fish, poultry and game — 28 oxen and 300 sheep daily to satisfy the lusty appetites of his master's guests!

He wrote his recipes on a vellum roll in 1390, and he called them "The Forme of Cury."

Although many of the ingredients are no longer obtainable — or even known — others are still familiar today but frequently used in an entirely different way.

Further recipes of 30 or 40 years later were collected and published by the English Text Society as "Two 15th Century Cookery Books." These, with another written in 1467 entitled "The Noble Boke Off Cookry," gave us a fascinating insight into the strange dishes — and appetites — of the Middle Ages!

Two important things stand out from these books — the extreme (and to modern tastes) nauseating use of spices, and the unusual methods of preparation.

In those times, no cook worth his salt would care — or dare — to serve a dish which tasted remotely like its main ingredients.

A simple stew, for example, or roast chicken, were absolutely

taboo, and as for the famous "Roast Beef of Olde England," that didn't come into favour until 200 years later.

Every dish, no matter how it began, finished up as nothing more than a succulent question mark.

For example, almost every one of the recipes in "The Forme of Cury," demanded the liberal use of ginger, sugar, and "gynger canel" (or cinnamon).

Saffron was another popular ingredient of the time. Made from the dried stamens of a form of crocus grown in Saffron Waldon, in Essex, it was used for both flavouring and for colouring. It dyes food a bright yellow, which was useful because in those days cooks prepared food as much to tickle the eye as the palate.

Pepper, mustard, nutmeg, cloves, cumin and coriander are still in use today but, in addition to these, the old cookery books prescribed honey, mace, minced dates, liquorice, buckwheat and

What Was Cooking 500 Years Ago?

Sugar and spice, things not so nice — you'd be surprised at just what went into the pot in the Middle Ages.

By KENNETH S. ALLEN

aniseed — as well as the less-familiar cubebs, saunders, verjuice and gromil.

When half a dozen or more of these had been liberally sprinkled in the pot — medieval cooks were never too precise about actual quantities — it's not surprising that the resulting taste bore little or no resemblance to the principal ingredients.

WHEN you study the actual preparation of the food, you immediately realise just how much muscular effort was involved. For the cook, or his scullions, were constantly told to "play it, hew it, grind it small as thou may."

There were two reasons for this. The diners had no forks — they weren't introduced to England until the reign of James I, and eating would have been both difficult and laborious with only a spoon and knife. Also, by pulping everything it was far easier to mix in the cubebs, ginger and other spices.

I would imagine that the pestle and mortar had pride of place in every well-run kitchen!

Here's an actual recipe, and just look at the amount of strong-arm work that was needed to prepare "Coffins." They are pastry cases made to contain the food.

"Take veal and smite it in little pieces into a pot and wash clean.

"Then take fair (clean) water and let it boil together with parsley, sage, savoury and hyssop cut small enough, and when it is boiling take powdered pepper, cinnamon, cloves, mace, saffron, and let them boil together, and a good deal of wine wherewith.

"When the flesh is boiled, take it from the broth all clean, and let the broth cool; and when it is cold, take eggs, the white and the yolks, and cast through a strainer, and

37

put them into the broth, so may that the broth be stiff enough.

"Then make fair coffins and couch pieces of the flesh in a coffin. Then take dates and cut them, and cast thereto. Then take powdered ginger and a little verjuice, and put into the broth and salt. And then put the broth into the coffins, bake a little with the flesh before thou put thy liquor thereon, and let all bake together till it be enough (done)."

IT is wrong, however, to think that our medieval ancestors spent all their lives at a groaning table. Far from it.

During the winter when food was needed most, many of the households had to live on very plain fare. Every year, as the autumn mists fell over the country and pasture became scarce, a great slaughter began.

Beef, pork and fish were salted and stored away in casks until needed.

There were no potatoes to help the diet, and the cabbage, leeks and onions that struggled through the winter were sorry specimens.

But when spring came again, the first shy flowers took second place to thoughts of fresh meat and vegetables. I expect there was a great loosening of belts as the good trencherman looked forward to months of plenty!

What activity there must have been in those great, stone kitchens as the chief cooks took down their cookery rolls, or sat in their privileged seat nearest the fire, and dreamed up fresh ways of disguising basic ingredients.

Many of the best combined culinary dexterity with real artistry. To this was added downright inventiveness, for the "suttelties" (or edible centrepieces) were the highspots of the great banquets and were greeted with cries of wonder.

There were sugar creations representing churches with stained-glass windows; castles surrounded by moats and besieging armies and so on.

At the Coronation feast of Henry V, for example, there were two dozen swans, antelopes and eagles of gold, all with mottoes in their mouths bearing such loyal messages as, "Noble honour and joy," "D'est jour notable et Honorable," and others in the same strain.

"Suttelties" were announced by a flourish of trumpets and carried through the banqueting hall in stately procession. Some were so beautiful that it must have really upset the cook to see his masterpiece fall before the knives and spoons of the attacking guests!

IT is almost with a feeling of relief that we leave these over-spiced and heavily-pulverised dishes and feast our eyes on those of a more gracious period.

A notable book was published in 1656 under the forbidding title of "Archimagirus Anglo-Gallicus."

Written by a Dr Mayerne and dedicated to the unfortunate Queen Henrietta Maria, it gives a fascinating picture, not only of the meals, but also of the manners, customs and social graces of the court of Charles I.

The book is divided into three parts.

The first is entitled "The Queen's Closet Opened," the second, "A Queen's Delight or the Art of Preserving, Conserving and Candying," and the third, and most interesting of all, "The Compleat Cook."

This was followed by two more books, both of which were brought out in 1671, the "Accomplished Cook" by Robert May and "The Closet of the Eminently Learned Sir Kenelm Digby, Kt., Opened." The latter is particularly interesting, as Sir Kenelm includes recipes subscribed by many of the aristocrats and distinguished personalities of the time.

The year 1700 saw the publication of "The Art of Cookery" by William King, and it is interesting to note that all great cookery books of this period — those of Mayerne and Digby, May and King — were all written by doctors. Not one is by a practising chef, as one would expect — and not one by a woman.

Even the "Art of Cookery Made Plain and Easy," a best-seller of the time and written under the name of Mrs Hannah Glasse, was actually the work of another doctor — Dr Hill.

Although the authorship may have been debatable, its popularity was never in doubt. "Her" preface shows a commendable pro-British outlook, and after referring to "those French gentry who pretend to be better cooks than Britons," it attacks the popular belief that English dishes tasted better for being given French names!

The forthright Dr Johnson must have known who lurked behind the pseudonym, for he declared on several occasions that no women could ever write a cookery book.

Then, in 1846, came the cookery book that was destined to revolutionise the art in England.

Called the "Gastronomic Regenerator," it was the work of Alexis Soyer, considered to be the greatest of all chefs.

With it, he swept away the last of the strange recipes and notions that still persisted after 500 years. Modern cooking had arrived.

TODAY, alas, many of the old books have little practical value. The days when the cook was instructed to "take the yolks of a large number of eggs, newly-laid," have gone.

But dieting and balanced meals are by no means something new. Far from it.

The first great book on the subject was attributed to Aristotle and was called "Secret of Secrets." This was popular in Britain for nearly 500 years.

An interesting reflection upon the state of some rivers, lakes and ponds of those days is the old writer's constant harping upon the subject of drinking water.

"Secret of Secrets" says, "Whoever drinks water whilst eating or immediately after, extinguishes in himself the natural heat and troubles the digestion by corrupting the foods that have been taken."

Tudor medicinal books have something further to say on the subject.

"To drink between meals is not laudable," Sir Thomas Elyot says in his "Castel of Helth" (1534) "except very great thrist constraineth, for it interrupteth the office of the stomach in concoction (digestion) and causeth the meat to pass faster than it should do . . ."

Yet, despite their quaint mode of expression, these books contain much that is in keeping with modern practice.

It is refreshing to think that, despite the gargantuan meals of the past, the trencherman did give some thought to his hard-working stomach.

All things considered, they must have done very well. In fact, the only recipe that their old books omitted was:

"Take onne spoone of ye Bicarbonate of Soda . . ." ■

Complete Story by VERA PROCTOR

MY bedroom faced the fields, away from the housing estate, so that the first light of morning came through my window. I'd lain in bed and watched the day lighten minute by minute. Now I could see my wardrobe standing out as if it were the only piece of furniture in the room.

Lying perfectly still, I imagined myself opening the door of the wardrobe and touching my wedding dress — a cloud of white I had thought I would never wear.

By this time tomorrow . . . By this time tomorrow I would no longer be Kim Miller. What would it be like to wake up in a room a hundred miles away, a room that faced the sea . . . as Mrs Nick Paterson?

Nick — the very thought of him set my heart pounding. I'd loved him for as long as I could remember.

As a little girl I used to sprawl on the grass with the other kids from the estate and watch as Nick and his father came up from the "country," laden with their huge bundles of flowers.

The "country" — flat green land that ran from the estate to the skyline — was a mystery in those days. So was Nick.

He had stayed a stranger, too, until that wonderful day 10 months ago. At last, when I had almost given up hope, Nick noticed me in the way I had always dreamed . . .

I jumped out of bed and went to the window to look into the shimmering distance, to where I knew Nick would be. Lush greenery stretched silent and still.

Yet I wasn't content. Even today, the very day I was to become Nick's wife, I was still beset by doubts, nagged by jealousy.

For Nick had been in love before. I'd never, not even on the day he asked me to marry him, seen him look at me the way he used to look at Lucy Deane.

Lucy and her family were latecomers to the estate. I don't know where they came from, but it was obvious that 16-year-old Lucy was a town girl. She was blonde and witty and vastly more assured than any of the rest of us.

We were an easy-going group of youngsters, ready to welcome anyone who wanted to join us. At our meeting-place on the edge of the estate we would decide whether to go to the club, the café, or to take cycle rides into the country.

The very first time I saw Lucy stroll along and sit herself down among us, I knew things were about to change. Immediately the boys stopped being one of a crowd and became acutely self-conscious. Lucy had that effect on the opposite sex.

She was beautiful. Not merely pretty or attractive, but shiningly beautiful. She had the kind of poise that made the rest of us girls terribly aware that we had only just left school.

Lucy pounced on Nick with her eyes as soon as he came striding

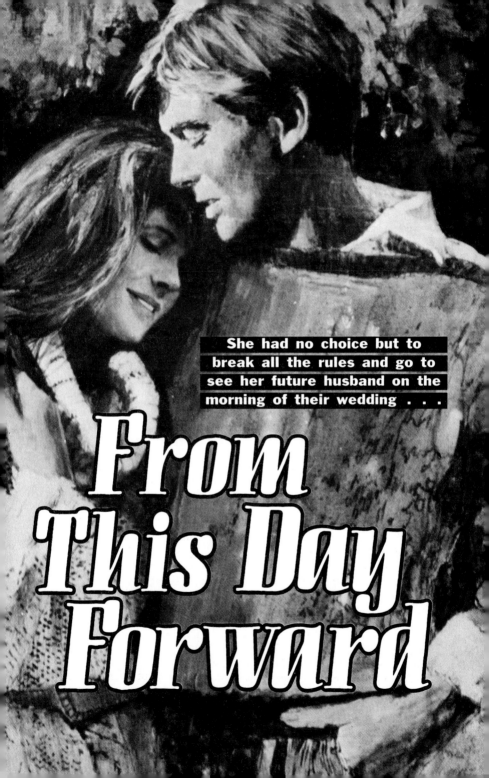

She had no choice but to
break all the rules and go to
see her future husband on the
morning of their wedding . . .

From This Day Forward

up the lane. Who could blame her? Nick, a year or so older than most of us, was so tall and vital, so good looking. And the way he looked at Lucy sent a spark of agony through my heart.

Jealousy is a mysterious thing, a seed which plants itself, grows deeply and demands constant attention. I gave into it by leaving home.

I went 30 miles away, to the coast, to work in a hotel. My parents considered me too young, but they could see I was unhappy at home.

I stepped into my new world, determined to keep secretly in touch with the old one. I listened eagerly to the rumours about the Deanes — that they were restless, in debt, gamblers even. I longed for the day when Lucy Deane would leave our town.

But when that day came, Nick went, too.

Nick's family owned a flower nursery in the country and rumour said he had gone away to learn more up-to-date business methods. But I lived in dread of hearing that he had married Lucy Deane.

THEN one day in August, 18 months later, I was standing at the staff entrance, blinking in the sunlight, when I saw Nick.

"So this is where you escaped to, Kim!" He smiled. "I've been home nearly a week — and missed seeing you around."

I stood and stared at him, unable to speak. My breath caught and my heart hammered in my ears. I felt his hand firm on my arm, and then we were running like children again, towards the beach.

We talked and talked until we'd caught up on all that had happened since I'd left. But Nick never once mentioned Lucy Deane and I could not bring myself to ask.

Nick was working hard at the nursery, laying out new flower-beds, but he bought a car and drove over to meet me whenever I was off duty.

We strolled along the pier in the misty autumn chill and sat in the car watching pale sunshine on the water on November mornings.

We joined in the fun at the hotel when Christmas came, and a fortnight before Easter Nick came to drive me home for a short holiday.

Half a mile before the town, he swung suddenly to the right and took the road that led up to the Downs. He stopped the car and looked out at the countryside spread around us, newly green and sweet. There was silence as the engine died, then Nick turned towards me.

In the moment before he took me in his arms I looked into his eyes, and my heart stood still.

"Kim . . ." he said softly, and then his lips were on mine.

Nick had kissed me before, but never as he did then. When I opened my eyes the sky was spinning crazily.

Swiftly Nick pulled me even closer. "I love you, Kim," he whispered. "I always have. Say you'll marry me."

I was so happy I cried. Laughing, Nick mopped up my tears until I was laughing too.

"AND I QUOTE ..."

Robert Morley (1908-), English actor and author, made his first appearance on the stage in 1928, and has achieved a great reputation, particularly in comedy. He has also written plays, and numerous articles for such magazines as *Punch*, *Tatler*, and *Playboy*.

⇨ *Most dog owners are at length able to teach themselves to obey their dog.*

⇨ *I have little patience with anyone who is not self-satisfied . . . The high spot of every day is when I first catch a glimpse of myself in the shaving mirror.*

⇨ *The show which, alas, every actor has to miss is his own memorial service.*

⇨ *To watch a Frenchman pay for something is to watch him die a slow death.*

Our parents were delighted and arrangements went swiftly and easily ahead. But Nick had still not said a word about Lucy Deane.

I PUSHED away from the window and began to dress furiously. I couldn't go on without knowing if he still loved her. No matter what happened I had to know . . .

As I crept from the house the estate began to come to life. I heard a car start up, a baby cry, a dog bark excitedly . . .

Skirting the houses, I ran up the lane. Nick was kneeling by the side of one of the flower-beds. When he heard me he leapt to his feet and held out his arms, and I ran into them.

"Darling!" he said, laughing. "Does your mother know? She'll think this is most unlucky. Seeing your future husband before the wedding!"

Would it be unlucky? For a moment, as we clung together, I wondered if I should keep quiet. For what if I should speak, and lose him? But for both our sakes, I must ask.

I swallowed desperately. "Darling," I said, "I'm sorry . . . but I just have to know. Did you really love Lucy Deane?"

Continued on page 46.

They say owls are wise birds — but what were we to do with a little bundle of fluff who, it seemed, just wouldn't behave like a good owl should?

By Mrs C.D. EAMES

A S stray or injured creatures invariably put themselves in the path of our children, I wasn't surprised when my son returned from a fishing trip with something wrapped in his sweater. What did surprise me was the enormity of the eyes that stared warily at me as I lifted the newcomer from the garment.

If you can imagine a large dandelion-clock, swamped by a pair of enormous, saucer-like eyes, then you'll have some idea of what our visitor looked like, and when I noticed the wide, hooked beak, I knew without any doubt that I was holding a fledgling owl.

Owls were no strangers to us living in the country. We had heard their callings, and on some occasions had seen them flitting through the night on large, silent wings. Yet that was the closest we had ever been to one — and one so young, too.

Looking at it, sitting in the palm of my hand and trembling slightly, I wanted to laugh at its very absurdity, but upon touching its fluffy body and feeling the delicate bone structure, I was saddened by its complete vulnerability. Had my son left it in the grass, it would have fallen prey to any passing stoat or weasel.

We had no experience of owl rearing, and books from the library offered little help on the subject, so we decided to play it by ear.

A grocery box lined with straw became his "nest," and he settled in remarkably well, although he would open his beak wide and menacingly whenever we put our hands near him — but as our hands usually held some tit-bit he soon grew used to being petted.

Bread and milk and hard-boiled eggs were his favourite food, but as he grew older I added meat to his diet — even though my stomach recoiled at the sight of a bird gulping down gobbets of raw meat, which left his beak bloody and gaping for more.

But he *was* an owl, and as raw meat is an owl's chief food, I knew that I would have to overcome my squeamishness if we were going to rear him successfully.

T HEN something began puzzling me. I had always believed that owls said, in sweet little voices,

TAWNY,
the owl who couldn't

"Tu whit tu whoo" or even "Kee-wick."

Our owl didn't. He only said, "Kraak!" in a voice that was anything but sweet!

I decided that his lack of hooting was due to the fact that he had never heard another owl, so the remedy was crystal clear — I would teach him.

Looking into his large black eyes, I hooted in what I hoped was a convincing manner, over and over again, day after day.

It was futile. He stared blankly and surprisedly (as did my friends), and said — as if you hadn't guessed — "Kraak!"

By the age of four months he had lost his thistledown look, and had acquired a coating of glossy feathers that shaded from the deepest chocolate to the palest grey.

The discs round his eyes had grown, too, making his eyes appear larger than ever. We knew then that he was a tawny owl — and named him accordingly.

Of course, he had graduated from the grocery box by that time, and his favourite perch was on my shoulder. There's many a household chore I've done as "Long John Silver" — much to the delight of any calling tradesman! However, an owl's talons are a deadly weapon, and as Tawny was growing fast, we had to wean him away from shoulders.

A broom handle placed between two chairs made a good substitute, and he would sit most of the day, watching the goings on, wearing his "wise owl" look.

What did worry me at that time was our family of cats, for

L. ARNOLD.

give two hoots...

although we took reasonable precautions regarding the owl's safety, we knew an accident could happen.

With plenty of help at hand, I decided to bring matters to a head. I'd confront the cats with the owl.

After I'd lured the cats into the room where Tawny was perched, we waited with bated breath.

He took one look at those feline shapes, then puffed himself out until he looked twice his normal size — and twice as forbidding.

"Kraak!" he said.

The cats needed no second telling — they fled en masse from the room in terror. I needn't have worried at all.

THE day Tawny discovered he could fly was quite eventful. In a series of flutters and flaps, he landed on the window ledge.

"Kraak!"

It was a cry of triumph. Outside, the day was sunny and fresh with the scents of summer. On impulse I carried him out and put him on the lowest branch of the pear tree.

With wings outstretched to the sun's warmth, he preened and shook his feathers, then with little bobbing steps he swayed along the branch, seemingly entranced by the birdsong all around him.

Then it happened. He fell out of the tree!

I felt as stunned as the owl. On examining him I found he had damaged a wing.

I could almost hear the laughter in the vet's voice, as it echoed down the phone, "Fell out of a tree, you say?" He advised me to take the owl into the next town, where there was a vet who was an expert on owls.

It wasn't the happiest of journeys. It's been my experience that if you take a box on a bus, and pitiful little "Meows" or whines emit from its confines, you'll meet with friendly and sympathetic smiles from your fellow travellers.

But you try taking a box on a bus and the only sound to be heard is "Kraak!" You'll be regarded with as much suspicion as if the sound was "Tick-tock-tick."

Any fond hopes I'd been nursing of having a cosy chat with that vet were doomed from the start, as he turned out to be a dour Scot who seemed to think that words were a superfluous commodity.

However, the Scot handled

Continued from page 43.

I closed my eyes and seemed to stop breathing as I waited for him to speak.

His arms drew me closer. I opened my eyes and a mist swam before them. When I looked up into Nick's face I saw that he looked puzzled.

"Lucy Deane," he repeated, and the line of his eyebrows drew together. Then his lips moved in a sad smile. "Poor little Lucy.

"She was so determined to have a good time she never stayed with anyone long enough to fall in love. When someone with more money came along she left me without even saying goodbye. And to tell the truth I was glad to see her go. I knew by then I'd never loved her."

He took my hand, led me to a gate, and we leaned against it.

"I shall always be grateful to Lucy," he went on softly. "I was

Tawny skilfully, and said that the damaged wing was nothing serious. Then!

"Ye canna' keep him!" I was fixed by a stare as cold as a Scottish burn. "And ye canna' turn him loose!"

It appeared that if we turned Tawny loose, he would perish. To keep him indefinitely was going against his wild nature. From the vet, I learnt that owls don't hunt their prey by instinct — they have to be taught, so until we were satisfied that our owl could catch and kill his own food, he must remain a captive.

Because of the increase in Tawny's already impressive wing span, we decided he needed more space. Our old pony was turned into the paddock, and the stable was turned into an aviary.

THE subject of his education arose again, and as the summer was almost over, we thought it would be a good thing to set him free before winter.

Thankfully, my husband elected to be tutor. I was so glad that he had undertaken to "train" the owl, for if, through squeamishness, we had let Tawny down on that last,

vital stage of his rearing, it would have been tantamount to signing his death warrant.

The fact that he had learnt his lessons quickly showed that he was ready to rejoin his own kind.

It was a cool night, musky with the scent of a garden bonfire. I lay awake, waiting for sleep to come, when I heard it. From the aviary came the beloved "Kraak!" then, from a nearby tree, "Tu whit tu whoo."

I shook my husband awake. In the dim light, we could just make out the shape of a visiting owl. The calling went on for several minutes, then from the aviary came the clearest "Tu whoo-oo." Our owl had done it — and it had taken a love greater than the one I could offer.

That was all it needed. We put Tawny in the pear tree just after sunset the next evening. He stayed motionless for a long time, then slowly spread his wings, and launched himself in a graceful sweep from the tree, gained height and circled the rooftop twice.

Then he melted away into the night, leaving a final "Whoo-oo" and an empty stable to remind us that he had ever been. ■

---

young and mixed up about life and love.

"Lucy helped me to sort myself out," he said softly. "If she hadn't — " He spread his hands. "I might not have recognised true love, even now.

"It's you I love, Kim," he said simply. "Today and for always."

He said no more, but his eyes asked if I was satisfied.

I nodded, happily, truthfully. For in that moment I knew that jealousy was dead for ever, it had been banished by love.

Happiness swept through me.

I put my arms around his neck, stretched up and kissed Nick swiftly. Then I turned and rushed back up the lane.

I ran home as fast as I could. To get ready for my wedding.

———— * **THE END** * ————

SADIE NORTHCOTT woke up at her usual time, just as the tea trolley clattered into the ward. She lay quietly, half propped-up on her pillows, watching the summer light filter through the windows and trying to listen for the birds.

She hadn't heard any birds for so long, not since she'd been found on the floor of her cottage in spring and taken to the geriatric ward. She knew there were birds in the city and surely some of them would sing now. Somehow she was convinced that today she would hear birdsong.

There was something different about today — something special. She could feel the summer in herself; her legs weren't aching quite so badly and her thin, frail hands lying on the top sheet weren't shaking. And there was something else, too — she couldn't place what it was and her tired mind ranged over possibilities.

Was Margaret coming today? Or maybe that nice hospital visitor who was so often there to fill the gap of absent relatives and friends?

Was Nurse Tomkin on duty with her light step and deft hands and smiling blue eyes?

She closed her eyes and tried to gather her thoughts together. No, her sense of anticipation had nothing to do with any of those possibilities. It was something to do with birdsong.

She lifted her head with difficulty and tried to listen hard with her good, left ear, but it was no good.

Nurse Derry was rolling some screens around Mrs White's bed and calling loudly:

"Time for a wash, Mrs White!"

Sadie lay back, smiling. It didn't matter because she knew something nice was going to happen.

It was like the times when she had woken as a child to the subconscious knowledge of a birthday. Or later 60 years ago, when she had counted the days to Matthew's next leave.

She fixed her faded eyes on the pearly sky outside the tall windows and waited . . .

SAMANTHA DERRY was not happy that morning. She was working three nights a week at the City General Hospital to help with the mortgage and the cost of the car, and by the end of the second night she was always over-tired and irritable.

Of course, once Tina started school she could get more rest during the day and it would be easier then. But at the moment, the local

The Old Lady

And to think, one nurse actually felt sorry for her — she, who had the most precious gift of all ...

Complete Story by SUSAN SALLIS

In Bed Four

nursery school was full and her mother could no longer baby-sit since she, too, had started a part-time job.

Really, it was all a bit too much.

Last night had been nearly the last straw.

She had settled Tina by seven o'clock and was dashing around getting ready to leave the house in good time when Don started teasing her and chasing her about, acting like an irresponsible 20-year-old instead of a husband and father of nearly 30.

She had rounded on him suddenly.

"Look, Don," she'd said fiercely, "if you've got time to act the fool, kindly do it on your own. I don't enjoy going out to work when everyone else is settling down to watch television, you know. And you're not making it any easier!"

His hands had tightened on her waist. "Sam, darling . . . you don't have to work."

"I don't have to work?" For one dreadful moment she could have hit him.

"How would we run the car if I didn't work? How would we have bought the suite? Or the bedroom carpet? Or — "

His hands had dropped to his side. "We don't have to run the car, Sam. I could walk to work — "

"Three miles?"

"It wouldn't hurt me. And at the weekend — we could go for walks then, too."

"All right, forget the car. But what about the other luxuries my money pays for?" she'd asked.

"Luxuries. That's the right word, isn't it?" He had looked at her with unaccustomed seriousness.

"We can do without luxuries, Sam. We've got something else."

She'd known what he meant but she misunderstood him — deliberately.

"Does that mean I have to ditch my career? Nursing isn't just any old job," she'd said firmly.

He'd looked impatient. "You can go back to it, Sam. There are plenty of other people who can look after old people — "

"Geriatric work isn't real nursing — is that what you mean?" she'd interrupted fiercely.

His eyes dropped and he'd said wearily:

"No, of course not, love. I was only suggesting you postpone your career until Tina is older. But, of course, if that's what you want . . ."

She had wanted to tell him that she didn't know just what she wanted any more. But there wasn't time. She was on duty at eight o'clock and it was already seven-thirty. So she ran.

NOW as the end of her night shift approached, she looked down the long ward and wondered what it was all about. Nursing old people seemed such a hopeless sort of a job. She couldn't do a thing for them that anyone else couldn't do equally well. Keep them clean, feed them. Anyone could manage that without three years' training.

"Come along, Mrs White," she said, trying to be cheerful. "Time for your wash."

She clanked the screens noisily across the floor and made a start to her first patient.

By the time she got to the top of the ward she was ready to drop. She reached the old lady in bed four and stopped.

Sadie Northcott was looking out of the window, a half-smile on her face.

Her early-morning tea was untouched on the locker and it was plain she was miles away.

Samantha paused a moment, staring at her, and then a chill ran through her as she thought that one day she would be like this. Sadie had a friend who came to visit her once every two or three weeks, otherwise — nothing, no children, no relatives.

Her eyes tired quickly reading a newspaper or watching television, and her hearing wasn't too good either.

Samantha sighed. She must live entirely on memories.

Samantha took the frail hands in hers and washed and dried them carefully.

"Try to drink your tea, Mrs Northcott," she said, offering her the cup.

She declined with a slight shake of her head.

Samantha sighed. "I don't know what's wrong with you. You must be in love, Mrs Northcott!" she said quickly and clanked the trolley back the way she had come to where the day staff were already taking over.

Nancy Tomkin, her blue eyes clear and sparkling at this hour of the morning, opened the doors for Samantha then called to the long row of beds:

"Sleep well, girls?"

A few answered her and in bed four Mrs Northcott waved almost excitedly.

"Hey, what have you been doing to our Sadie?" Nancy asked as she followed Samantha into the kitchen. "She looks very lively."

"I don't know," Samantha said and sat down on a chair. "Have you noticed that all they talk about is the past?" She paused. "But who can blame them? That's all they've got, isn't it?"

Nancy looked surprised. "Hey, that's not like you, Samantha," she said. "Look, I know it's hard and we can only do our best.

"Now, I think it's time you called it a day. You get home and get some sleep, my girl," she went on briskly.

"I'll see you at eight tonight and you'll be full of enthusiasm while I'm on my last legs."

Samantha shook her head wearily and watched with something like envy as Nancy disappeared through the swing doors and she caught a glimpse of the patients' smiles of welcome.

Continued on page 55

There's no need to be an expert chef — just gather together some simple ingredients and you and your family can look forward to titbits and main meals with —

Variety & Spice

VOL-AU-VENTS

| 170 g tin Plumrose Bacon Grill |
| 250 ml milk |
| 25 g flour |
| 25 g butter |
| 2 teaspoonfuls tomato purée |
| 4 level tablespoonfuls condensed cream of celery soup |
| Ready-made vol-au-vent cases |

● Pour the milk into a saucepan and whisk in the flour. Add the butter and cook, stirring continuously until the sauce boils, thickens and is smooth.

Blend in the tomato purée. Cover and set aside to cool.

Beat in the celery soup. Chop the Bacon Grill into tiny pieces and fold in. Spoon into the vol-au-vent cases.

52

PLUMROSE PIZZAS

| 113 g packet (4 slices) Plumrose Cooked Ham, cut into thin strips |
| 113 g (8 slice packet) Plumrose Danish Salami, chopped |
| 2 x 20 cm frozen pizza bases |
| 1 onion, finely chopped |
| 15 g butter |
| 397 g tin chopped tomatoes |
| 1 level teaspoonful dried mixed herbs |
| Pinch mixed spice |
| Salt and pepper, to taste |
| ½ teaspoonful sugar |
| 3 level teaspoonfuls cornflour |
| 100 g cheese, grated |

RITZY RISOTTO

300 g tin Plumrose Chopped Ham with Pork, finely chopped

150 g long grain rice

100 g Gouda cheese, grated

Black pepper

100 g salted peanuts, finely chopped

Lettuce leaves

● Cook the rice in boiling salted water until tender. Drain and put into a bowl.

While still piping hot, add the grated cheese and season with black pepper, stir until the cheese begins to melt.

Allow to cool slightly before folding in the ham and chopped nuts.

Line a salad bowl with lettuce and pile the risotto in the middle.

SAUSAGE SALAD

6 Plumrose Hot Dog Sausages, sliced

2 large pickled gherkins, sliced

100 g cooked sweetcorn

1 unpeeled eating apple, cored and diced

Bunch radishes, thinly sliced

3 tablespoonfuls salad oil

1½ tablespoonfuls wine vinegar

1 teaspoonful made mustard

Pinch salt, pepper and sugar

● Mix together the sausages, gherkins, sweetcorn, apple and radishes and put into a salad serving bowl.

Put the remaining ingredients into a screw-top jar and shake vigorously.

Fold into the salad and serve.

2 tablespoonfuls chopped fresh or frozen peppers

Few black olives, pitted

Small tin pineapple pieces

● Remove wrapping from the pizza bases and place on baking sheets.

Gently cook the onion in the butter until soft but not brown. Drain juice from the tomatoes and place in a jug. Set aside. Add the tomatoes, herbs and spice to the onion. Simmer for 5 minutes. Season with the salt, pepper and sugar.

Blend the cornflour and tomato juice together and stir into the tomato mixture. Bring to the boil, stirring, until the mixture is very thick.

Spread the sauce over the pizza bases and sprinkle the cheese over.

On one pizza, arrange the pepper and salami. Garnish with the black olives.

On the remaining pizza, arrange the pineapple and cooked ham.

Bake for 20 minutes at 425 deg. F., 220 deg. C., Gas Mark 7.

53

DEVILLED FRANKFURTERS

227 g tin Plumrose Party
Sausages, drained

1 onion, thinly sliced

25 g butter

125 ml sour cream

2 teaspoonfuls made mustard

Salt and pepper

● Cook the onion slices in the butter until soft but not brown.

Cut the sausages in half diagonally and add to the onion.

Stir in the sour cream and mustard and cook gently for 3 or 4 minutes until the sausages are heated right through.

Season to taste and serve piping hot with crusty bread.

LASAGNE

2 x 227 g packets Plumrose
Cooked Ham, cut into 1-inch
pieces

15 g butter

1 onion, finely chopped

397 g tin chopped tomatoes

1 level tablespoonful tomato
purée

2 level teaspoonfuls dried mixed
herbs

Salt and pepper

¼ teaspoonful sugar

200 g carton soft cheese

125 ml carton natural yoghurt

100 g pre-cooked lasagne verdi

150 g cheese, grated

● Put the butter into a saucepan and add the chopped onion. Cook gently until soft but not brown.

Stir in the chopped tomatoes, tomato purée, cooked ham and herbs. Cook, uncovered for 10 minutes. Season to taste with the salt, pepper and sugar.

Blend the soft cheese and yoghurt together until smooth and creamy.

Pour half the tomato and ham into the lasagne dish. Cover with a single layer of half the lasagne then spread half the soft cheese and yoghurt mixture on top. Cover with the remaining tomato and ham, a layer of lasagne and the remaining soft cheese. Cover with foil and cook at 375 deg. F., 190 deg. C., Gas Mark 5, for 45 minutes.

Remove the foil and cover with a thick layer of grated cheese. Continue cooking until just melted.

HAM GOUGERE

300 g tin Plumrose Cooked Ham,
cut into ½-inch cubes

50 g butter

65 g plain flour, sifted on to a
plate

2 eggs, beaten

125 ml mayonnaise

125 ml plain yoghurt

1 level tablespoonful apricot jam

2 level teaspoonfuls curry powder

● Cut the butter into pieces and put into a small saucepan with 125 ml cold water. Bring to the boil.

Remove from the heat and as soon as the bubbles have subsided, add the flour all at once. Stir until the mixture forms a ball and leaves the sides of the pan. Tip into a mixing bowl and allow to cool for 2 minutes.

Using an electric whisk, beat in the egg a little at a time. Beat for about 3 minutes until glossy and stiff enough to hold its own shape.

Spread a little of the mixture in a thin layer on the bottom of a greased 1-litre pie dish. Pipe or fork the remaining mixture round the edge of the dish and bake for 25-30 minutes at 425 deg. F., 220 deg. C., Gas Mark 7, until golden brown and crisp. Allow to cool.

Blend the mayonnaise, yoghurt, apricot jam and curry powder together. Fold in the cubes of ham and pile into the gougère case.

Continued from page 51
SADIE had never seen the ward so full of light. The minute Nurse Derry switched off the long, overhead tubes, sunshine bathed everything, making it quite beautiful.

Even Miss Hargreaves in the next bed, sitting up there frowning as usual, was haloed by it.

It reminded Sadie of the time Matthew had held a buttercup beneath her chin and laughed.

"My goodness, you like butter, Sadie-girl," he'd said, then touching her neck, had gone on, suddenly serious:

"You've got a beautiful neck, too — did you know that?"

Sadie lay back and half-closed her eyes, smiling. So silly to think anything had changed, anything was over. She was the same inside herself as she had always been and so was everyone else. It only needed a ray of sunshine to remind her.

Nurse Derry was washing her. She was conscious of the efficient hands, the firm but gentle touch. Neither of them spoke and Sadie felt as if this beautiful girl was part of the sunshine. Perhaps that was the reason for her sense of anticipation?

Nurse Derry was bending over her, holding out her cup. Sadie shook her head, smiling, knowing that Nurse Derry would understand she couldn't be bothered with tea just now.

The cup disappeared and Nurse Derry's voice, high-pitched to break through Sadie's deafness, said, "You must be in love, Mrs Northcott."

Then there was a swish of starched apron as she went back up the ward behind her trolley.

Sadie lay still while realisation flooded through and through her and she almost gasped at the sheer simplicity of it — at her own, stupid blindness throughout the past few months when she had lain here feeling that everything was finished.

Even the sunshine reminding her of buttercups and Matthew's admiration hadn't shown her. Her mind had told her to listen for the song of a bird, but it hadn't told her why. Now she knew.

Nurse Derry had told her. She was in love.

It was plain commonsense she was in love. When Matthew had known he was dying he had told her:

"Our love will go on, Sadie-girl. Love is eternity."

And she had accepted it, believed it.

And yet . . . and yet . . . she had forgotten how to feel the joy of love, the wonder of it, the terrific sense of excitement, so that anything could be just around the corner, anything at all.

She raised her head from the pillow. Waveringly, as if in a mirage, she could see Nurse Derry talking to Nurse Tomkin.

Nurse Tomkin said something and Sadie waved, hoping that Nurse Derry would see and come back. But the two girls went out.

It didn't matter. She would see them again and meanwhile she had so much to do. So much to think about . . .

Continued on page 56.

HEATHERS TO BLOOM ALL

DOES the word Heather make you think only of stretches of purple moorland in the early autumn?

Well, it needn't. For even a small garden can grow heaths that'll be in bloom every month of the year. And you can have colours from white through all shades of rose to purple, with green, copper and golden foliage.

If you're pressed for space, the smaller kinds can be grown in the rock garden. The winter flowering ones are particularly useful here, giving a glow to the garden on cold, bleak days.

Heathers won't mind if your soil is poor and sandy, as long as you tuck some peat around their roots,

and they will settle happily for a fibrous loam. But stiff, cold clay won't please them.

Where heathers are being massed, most varieties should be planted about two feet apart. Then when they are established they will join up, and smother the weeds.

The only attention they need is the trimming of faded flowers. This

An old tree stump provides a natural effect.

Continued from page 55.

MATTHEW NORTHCOTT was like no-one else she knew. He had lived in the village all his life — just as she had — and he worked on the home farm like her brothers and her father, but he was so different.

He could talk — about things neither of them had ever seen, and he could make them real. The first time he asked her father whether he could walk her to chapel, she was only 16 and he was 18, young and idealistic.

On the way home he told her about a book he was reading, something to do with the Roman Legions who had camped on this very land on their way to London.

And she had become so interested that when they heard cartwheels on the road and he had hissed, "Chariots! Quick, down in the ditch!" she had leaped down with him.

Luckily it was high summer and the ditch was dry.

Six months later when the First War had broken out he'd come to her.

"I've joined up, Sadie-girl," he said. "Will you wait for me?"

Sadness had hit her like a physical blow.

"Why, Matthew?" she'd asked. "You don't need to. Agricultural workers are needed just as much as soldiers. I heard Dad saying so the other day — "

"Old men, young boys, women . . . they can all work the land,

56

YEAR ROUND

Add a touch of moorland magic to your garden with a selection of beautiful heathers.

Don't forget the value of varieties noted for foliage colour rather than flower-power.

can be done yearly in the spring, or throughout the year, after individual plants have finished blooming.

There is no end of lovely varieties to choose from, but just now I'm only going to tell you about those

By FLORENCE BASTIE

I've grown myself.

Calluna vulgaris can vary from neat little six-inch clumps to long, elegant stems. The blooming period is from July until about October.

I grew two double-flowering kinds which were a source of constant pleasure — Alba plena with long spikes of pure white miniature rosettes, and H.E. Beale to match in silvery pink.

Quite different was Nana compacta. It's a baby one and is like a deep-green pin-cushion studded with dainty pink flowers.

Continued on page 58.

Sadie-girl. I've *got* to go. *Because* of the land. I can't let down everyone else who's gone to fight for it. *You* understand."

She had nodded, feeling 10 years older than when she had woken that morning.

Matthew had shown her by then that the past made the present, and the present made the future and all three went on for ever. So you had to do the best you could because nothing was forgotten in eternity.

But it had been hard to remember all that when he came home on leave. He had lost the knack of conversation and his eyes were haunted and he walked by her side as if he were a ghost.

On the last night of his leave they'd passed the spot where last year the squire's cart had become a Roman chariot for them.

She reminded him of it, hoping that the laughing happiness which had been almost tangible then would return.

His defences crumbled abruptly, and he'd said:

"Oh, Sadie, Sadie-girl. None of that has any meaning now. Why did they fight to keep the land safe if it had to end like this? There's no honour or glory in the trenches, my darling, just mud and rats."

He was 19 and she 17 and they had to find the wisdom of the ages very quickly. She put her arms around him and held him tightly as if she could protect him from the world.

"They had to think of other things, Matthew — like you must. You

Continued on page 58.

Continued from page 57.

I like the Irish Heaths, Daboecia, for their contrast in flower and leaf. They have glossy leaves and large, urn-shaped flowers.

They like a moist position and look pretty with ferns. According to variety, they bloom from May to September. The two I grew had white flowers with bright green foliage and glowing crimson with dark green.

THE Erica family is a large one, and E. Carnea is one of the hardiest. It doesn't object to a bit of lime in the soil. The flowers are out from December to April and make a cheerful addition to any garden. If you have nowhere else suitable, find room for a couple in front of a mixed border.

The variety Winter Beauty will reward you with sprays of rich pink bells in time for a Christmas table decoration.

Flower shapes among the heathers vary quite a lot, and E. Ciliaris is distinctive with pale green, downy foliage and pitcher-shaped bells in clusters. It flowers from July to October.

Late summer is the time when E. Vagans, the Cornish Heather, comes in for a bit of admiration. Rightly so, as the upright spikes of tightly-packed bells resemble bottle brushes — and as they fade, the flower heads turn a russet colour.

I grew two kinds very successfully on quite a heavy soil and they made lush growth — Lyonese with white flowers and brown anthers, a striking contrast, and Mrs D. F. Maxwell, a rich cherry pink.

If you choose your varieties with care, you can have a heather out in bloom every month in the year. ■

Continued from page 57.

must think of us . . . Sadie and Matthew. And other Sadies and Matthews still not born yet. That's how they did it, Matt. And that's how we'll do it," she'd said, defiantly.

There had been a silence while she felt him slowly stiffen, and then the summer dusk was broken by the clear, haunting note of a nightingale. She felt quickened by excitement and felt the same excitement begin in him.

"Matt," she'd whispered exultantly, " 'tis a nightingale — singing for us."

"Promising that we'll be all right . . . like a rainbow . . ." he added, joyfully.

"When this is over we'll get married, Sadie-girl. We'll raise a family and tell them about Roman Legions and nightingales . . ."

SADIE'S smile trembled a little now as she remembered their family, their two sons, Gordon and Frederick, killed in action in North Africa.

She remembered the long decade after the Second War when she and Matthew had grown old together and had forgotten the gift of spontaneous joy which had been theirs for so long.

The smile steadied again as she acknowledged her good fortune in finding the gift again, now, and she opened her eyes and looked into the worried blue gaze of Nurse Tomkin.

"Oh, Sadie — " The scolding voice was laughing at itself. "I was worried. I wondered where on earth you'd got to. It's your morning for the physiotherapist. Had you forgotten?"

Funny how all the nice things were happening today. Nurse Tomkin and the massage lady . . . perhaps Margaret would visit this afternoon.

"Where is Nurse Derry?" she whispered.

"Now, you know she's gone off duty, Sadie. I'm here if you want something. What is it?"

Sadie smiled and moved her head on the pillow. "I . . . want to thank her. Tonight . . ."

"Yes, tonight. Are you all right, Sadie? No, don't try to talk, dear. I'll fetch Sister. Maybe we'd better give your massage a miss today."

Sadie smiled and closed her eyes again. The sun was warm on her face and she let herself think of Gordon and Fred and the three-legged race in the buttercup field on village sports day.

"They'll win," Matthew had said confidently. "No need to jump up and down, Sadie-girl. Where's your dignity?"

"I must have mislaid it when I started going out with you, Matt Northcott!" she'd told him, waving her hat above her head as Fred and Gordon raced through the buttercups.

"Ay, I reckon so," Matt had replied mock-sadly. "Just stand still then while I see if you likes butter."

And he'd held a flower beneath her chin.

"Don't you even want to watch your sons win?" she'd asked tartly, trying to dodge the tickling petals.

"I know they'll win, even if they lose this race."

She tore her eyes from the boys and looked at him. He could be serious in the midst of laughter and this was his way of letting her know not only about his love and pride in his sons but — what must come first for him — the most important thing in his life . . . his love for his wife.

He'd turned it off immediately. "My goodness, you like butter, Sadie-girl . . . and you've got a beautiful neck, too."

Mingling with the cheering villagers as Fred and Gordon had broken the tape, Sadie could hear Sister's voice, sharply anxious.

"Mrs Northcott? Are you going to wake up and try to take a drink, dear? You've had nothing to eat today and it's tea-time."

"Not thirsty," Sadie whispered, opening her eyes and smiling as she realised that the past and present definitely were the same, so the future must be right here as well.

"Is Nurse Derry there?"

"No." Sister smiled back. "But you've got a visitor."

Of course, it was Margaret, her old friend and neighbour. Hadn't Sadie known everything nice would happen today? She took a hand almost as frail as her own and the two women sat in silent communion.

That afternoon Samantha managed to sleep for four hours while her neighbour took Tina for a walk with her own children.

Continued on page 62

As Others

THE UNEXPLAINED FILE

The film "ET" gave us a whimsical look at an encounter between an alien and our world, but what about documented sightings of UFOs? Ninety per cent. of them are easily explained — here **BETTY PUTTICK** examines the *other* ten per cent.

See Us?

THE other day two young men driving through the Hertfordshire countryside saw a strange object hovering high above them. It was unusual enough to make them stop the car and jump out, grabbing a camera they happened to have with them, and before it shot over their heads and disappeared rapidly, they were able to take several pictures of what resembled a huge, misty Mexican sombrero.

It's the classic UFO story — and perhaps it has happened to you?

During 1976, the British UFO Research Association received about 400 reports of sightings.

"Out of those, probably only about fifty can be said to be genuinely unidentifiable," Norman Oliver, Editor of the British UFO Research Association Journal, stressed.

"UFO sightings come in what we call 'flaps,' " he told me, "when an extraordinarily large number are reported.

"It usually happens when there have been a number of news reports in the Press, or something on TV, and people tend to look up and see things that seem unusual to them. But often there's a normal explanation.

"Only about ten per cent. of

Continued from page 61

sightings are really inexplicable, and we find this percentage is the same worldwide among UFO societies everywhere."

Well, during the early months of 1977 the British UFO Research Association had more reports of UFO sightings than during the whole of the previous year, many of these coming from a twenty-five-mile area around Milford Haven.

I don't think anyone admits to an encounter with little green men, but a seven-foot, silver-clad giant put "the fear of the Devil" into Pauline and Billy Coombs when he appeared at the window of their remote Welsh farmhouse, apparently fascinated by their television.

It happened there in 1978 when there was a flock of eye-witnesses'

reports from Pembrokeshire of flying objects of various kinds. Pauline Coombs was first driving down a lane when she was followed by a "flying football-shaped object which glowed with light. All the electrics in my car cut out," she said, "but when I told my husband he wouldn't believe me."

However, he too saw the silver-suited giant, and like his wife, found the encounter distinctly scary.

Another farmer's wife in the St Bride's Peninsula area of Pembrokeshire looked out early one morning to find a "forty-foot-wide, fifteen-foot-high UFO shaped like an upturned jelly mould" parked in the front garden.

"It was not a reflection, it actually obscured my view of the greenhouse. It was very lightweight

---

Continued from page 59

When she dished up the evening meal, she felt much better and wished, somehow, she could bridge the gap between Don and herself. But the only way to do so seemed to be by admitting that he was right and her nursing job could be done by plenty of others.

After they'd eaten she did say tentatively:

"Once our holiday is over, Don, I might ask Sister to replace me."

But he just looked over his newspaper with a closed face.

"Forget what I said last night, Sam," he told her. "I don't want you to feel like some slave around the place — that's no good for anybody."

SO she clattered dishes and put Tina to bed as usual and flew out of the house at seven-thirty. If only her work *were* as satisfying as she made out, the difficulty at home wouldn't be so bad. But it seemed she was neither a good nurse nor a good wife.

She almost dreaded taking over from Nancy, seeing her cheerful face and hearing the personal farewells she made to the patients.

However, when she got to the hospital, Nancy wasn't in the ward, or in the kitchen or Sister's office, or with the bevy of girls hurrying down the stairs.

Samantha started on the bedtime drinks, stacking the feeding cups on the trolley and filling the sugar bowl to the rim.

Then the door opened with a rush and Nancy stood there, her eyes red.

looking and silvery coloured," Mrs Josephine Hewison insisted.

And 14 primary school children in the same area also reported seeing a flying saucer. The headmaster, Mr Ralph Llewellyn, made them draw what they saw, and their sketches were remarkably similar.

"I find it difficult to accept that children of primary school age would be able to promote such a sustained and sophisticated hoax," he remarked.

IN May 1977, an experienced British Airways pilot, Captain Denis Wood, reported that on July 30, 1976, while flying his Trident to Portugal, he was asked by Lisbon Control to watch out for three mysterious objects that had appeared on their radar.

"We saw this very bright 'headlamp' in the sky," he said. "All the cabin staff saw it too. This bright light was joined by two cigar-shaped objects as big as battleships."

Many of the Trident's passengers saw the UFOs, which were also spotted by a British Airways Tri-Star below them, and a Portuguese aircraft, whose pilot reported that he had seen a bright light accelerating vertically in to the sky.

"Suggestions that these were balloons, satellites, strange clouds or reflections are quite unacceptable to us," Captain Wood said. "I wish someone could explain it to me."

Apparently they had kept quiet for nearly a year because they were afraid of ridicule. But surely UFOs have now achieved credibility

Continued on page 64

"Thank goodness you've come, Samantha, you were right — there's nothing for them, is there?"

Samantha stared in surprise. "What's wrong, Nancy — what's happened?"

"It's Sadie. She's dying . . . she's hung on all day to see you and thank you for something. I — " Nancy broke down.

Samantha comforted her as best she could. Then she stood up and straightened her cap. "She doesn't want to thank me, Nancy. I was a bit annoyed with her this morning. I feel so ashamed. I'll tell her I didn't mean it."

She walked down the long ward to Mrs Northcott's bed.

The old lady lay still, her eyes closed, the bedclothes reaching only to her waist so that her frail arms and neck looked like the crumpled stalks of buttercups.

Her eyes flickered instantly as Samantha closed the screens behind her. She smiled.

"You were right," Sadie whispered, haltingly.

Samantha kneeled quickly by the bed and put her face close to the barely-moving lips.

"I am in love. I was in love, so, of course, I am now. I'd just forgotten, and you reminded me. Thank you . . ."

Samantha stared down into the sunken eyes which she saw now were sky-blue like her own.

"I'm sorry," she said humbly. "I didn't know . . . I didn't realise . . ."

Continued on page 65

Continued from page 63

As Others See Us?

even if their actual nature and origin eludes us.

"Flying saucers" first flew into the orbit of the average citizen on June 24, 1947, when Kenneth Arnold, a businessman piloting his private plane near Mount Rainier in Washington, caught sight of nine disc-like objects skimming along at fantastic speed "as a saucer would if you skipped it across the water."

A newspaperman who interviewed Arnold used the expression "flying saucer." It passed into the language — and within weeks sightings of mysterious objects in the skies were reported all over the United States.

Since then, worldwide UFO spotters have described a wide variety of UFO shapes, sizes and colours.

They can apparently hover motionless, or follow aircraft or cars, but phenomenal acceleration well beyond our technology is a typical characteristic, and speeds of more than 10,000 m.p.h. have been recorded on radarscopes.

They disrupt car engines, television and radio, and on the sites of landings, scorched circles, withered grass and foliage and chemical changes in the soil have been found.

Obviously, some witnesses are really seeing weather balloons, meteors, satellites, ball lighting, the planet Venus or simply a charter flight for Majorca! But others may genuinely be seeing mysterious spacecraft of unknown origin.

Dr Felix Ziegel of the Moscow

Aviation Institute said at the 1967 Conference on Space Civilisations:

"In truth, Soviet radar has picked up unidentified flying objects for twenty years. We have well-documented sightings from every corner of the USSR. It's hard to believe that all are optical illusions. Illusions don't register clearly on photographic plates and radar."

So if UFOs are real, who's on board? One of the most interesting aspects of the current wave of UFO-ria is the landing of what the British UFO Research Association call "humanoids" — spacemen to you and me.

Of course, for years various-colourful characters have claimed personal contact with UFO crews, usually from Venus, apparently anxious lest we humble earthlings juggle our butterfingered way into nuclear war. It all sounds a bit like "Star Trek"! But the growing number of rather frightened people who allege they have actually been taken inside a UFO tell a more convincing story.

In the autumn of 1973, an epidemic of UFO reports swept America, beginning at the end of August, when sightings were reported in 22 areas of Georgia on the same night.

Then on October 12, United Press International transmitted this message:

"Pascagoula, Mississippi. Two shipyard workers who claim they were hauled aboard a UFO were taken to a military hospital on Friday to be checked for radiation.

"The Pressmen, UFO consultants and scientists who met Charles Hickson and Calvin Parker, found two frightened men. They had been fishing in the Pascagoula River on the evening of October 11 when a UFO emitting a blue light

Continued on page 66

64

Continued from page 63

Sadie smiled. "Of course you didn't. But you will. Something will happen and you'll realise."

There was a silence. Samantha took both hands in hers and held them warmly, then for some reason she put them against her face.

It was just at that very moment that she heard it.

It was incredible, but she knew it wasn't her imagination or a dream. As she knelt there, holding Sadie's hand and accepting that love was eternity, she heard the clear notes of a nightingale echoing through the ward.

When the bird stopped singing, Sadie had gone.

And Samantha no longer felt the sense of failure that had been disturbing her so much.

Very calmly she went about the sad business of death. It was nearly two hours later when she reached Miss Hargreaves and inquired:

"Miss Hargreaves, did you hear a bird singing just now? Before you had your cocoa?"

"A bird? In here? Do you think I'm going dotty, girl?"

Samantha smiled.

"Not *you*, Miss Hargreaves." She tucked the cover around the thin shoulders.

"Is there anything I can get you, dear?"

"No, thank you. I'll ring if there is." She looked grudgingly into the sky-blue eyes. "One thing about you, you answer the bells promptly enough. But don't call me dear!"

Samantha's smile widened then she passed Mrs Northcott's empty bed. She put her hand for a moment on the mattress, as if somehow, it might connect her again with that magical nightingale.

"Good night, girls," she called softly from the doors. "Ring if you want me. Sleep well."

A few hands were raised sleepily.

She went to the wall phone and dialled her own number.

"Sam? Is something wrong?" Don's voice was sharply anxious.

"No, nothing. I had to ring to tell you I love you, darling, so if I gave up work for a while how could I feel a slave?"

There was a pause, then he said slowly and warmly:

"You couldn't very well, could you?" His tone changed. "Darling Sam. I love you, too. Has anything happened?"

"Only that I've got some wonderful patients, Don. They deserve the best. And if I give up now I might come back a really good nurse."

"You're a good nurse already, Sam. Surely you knew that?" He sighed. "Anything else?"

"Yes. Don . . . I heard a nightingale tonight. In the ward. Behind some screens."

"You *must* be in love, my darling," he said huskily.

———————— * **THE END** * ————————

E

65

Continued from page 64

landed, and three 'grey creatures' emerged. One man fainted, and the other said, 'My arms just froze up and I couldn't move.' They were then 'floated aboard' and examined by something resembling a huge electronic eye.

" 'I just kept thinking,' one said, 'what if they'd carried us off? You'd have dragged the river and then forgotten about us.' "

Unknown to the two men, a tape recorder was left running while they were alone, and those who heard their conversation afterwards had no doubts that these men had genuinely gone through a shattering experience.

THEORIES about UFOs and where they come from are legion. Some believe they have a history going back to Biblical times or earlier, and references in the Bible and many ancient manuscripts are open to this interpretation.

It seams feasible that the glittering galaxy of space may contain other beings not unlike ourselves, but more advanced technologically.

Meantime, my only advice to you is — as they say in the advertisements — Watch This Space! ∎

UPDATE:

We still seem no nearer to understanding the UFO phenomenon, although in the past few years there have been many sightings and some new developments.

There have been hundreds of reports from around the world of triangular UFOs, usually very large with flashing red, green and white lights along the sides, and the expression, "as large as a football field," is often used.

These craft can hover motionless,

or accelerate abruptly to very high altitudes. In November, 1989, there were many reports over several days from Eupen, Belgium where people were frightened when the triangular craft flew very low over them.

Reports of a similar object flying over Brussels at the end of March, 1990 were corroborated by police patrols, and two fighter planes succeeded in circling it before it accelerated away.

At Easter more than 1000 people watched while the Belgian Air Force patrolled the skies in wait for the mysterious craft. It was seen, but it hovered so low that the planes were unable to make contact.

Russia experienced considerable UFO activity in 1989, including landings. On October 9, 1989, the Soviet News agency, TASS, reported the arrival of an alien craft in a park at Voronezh, about 300 miles south-east of Moscow, on September 27, in the evening. Some school children playing football and a number of adults saw a red, ball-shaped object hover, then descend, landing on four feet.

Three beings and what appeared to be a robot landed. They were between three and four metres tall, with small heads and luminous eyes, wearing silver suits and bronze-coloured boots.

Apparently, when one boy cried out, one of the aliens "froze" him with his eyes, and he pointed a "tube" he was carrying at another boy who vanished, re-appearing later when the craft had taken off. There is no report of the boy's reactions as his parents would not allow reporters to interview him.

There have been an increasing number of people claiming to have been taken aboard UFOs and sub-

Continued on page 69

HE hasn't always been "The Champ," of course. I can distinctly remember when he fitted nicely on my three-year-old daughter's lap. That was when visitors would "ooh" and "ah" over him, and tell him he was "sweet."

"He's terribly timid," we would explain, as he climbed up our skirts or trouser legs or hid his head under the nearest cushion.

HE'S THE CHAMP — AND I LOVE HIM !

As a puppy, Lucky was always ready to throw in the towel, says Elsie McCutcheon, but not any more — for as his four-footed rivals have discovered, he's a real knockout nowadays!

We called him, "Lucky," hoping he would be. However, during the next few months of our acquaintanceship, we thought of a few other names, which fitted him.

Such as "Glutton" (for there never was a greedier dog) or "Chewer" (for how long, we wondered, *did* dogs cut their teeth?) or just plain "Coward."

Eventually I became quite reluctant to take him for walks. Why? Because, at the advanced age of nine months, he still tried to jump up into my arms whenever he spotted another dog!

It was more than embarrassing — it was plain ludicrous.

I mean — how many housewives have you seen staggering along under the weight of a half-grown Boxer dog?

They hadn't seen many in our neighbourhood, anyway, I can vouch for that. My husband refused to be connected with such a cowardly cur and only my young daughter was sympathetic.

"He says they want to bite him," she proclaimed, after one of her long, intimate conversations with her "Lucky-Puppy," "and he's frightened to death!"

So that was that! What could one do, apart from try to reassure the neurotic beast, when it shook like a jelly and clawed your tights to ribbons in its panic?

And I've never forgotten the time when the workmen came to convert us to natural gas, and our bold Lucky was discovered quaking beneath the bed!

By ELSIE McCUTCHEON

AND so it went on, until our cowardly Boxer was well over a year old. Then, on one fine autumn morning, Lucky was actually attacked.

I don't know how he came to miss the other dog's approach. I'd seen it coming for quite five minutes, and so had my small daughter.

"Now he can make a friend!" I whispered to her.

How naive can you get! The approaching dog was an irascible, middle-aged cross-breed . . .

With a sudden, terrifying growling, howling bound, he was on our Lucky's back. Of course, when it was all over, there were three wrecks littering the roadway — a trembling, blood-spattered dog, a screaming child, and a quaking mother.

Lucky, we were relieved to find, hadn't been badly damaged. What we didn't realise was that he was a changed personality. "The Champ" had been born that day . . .

He started his new career the following day, and he used cats for target practice. Up till then he had run away from cats, as he ran away from everything and everybody, apart from the family.

Imagine my astonishment then, when, on spying a black cat on a garden wall, he set off at a gallop . . . in the direction of the cat!

Not only that, but he actually barked! The sound emitted was deep, masculine and, to judge from his expression, satisfying. The cat hopped it and Lucky returned.

I praised him enthusiastically but not too publicly, in case I was set upon by an indignant cat owner. There were three more cat chases before the end of that walk. The worm, we decided, had turned — with a vengeance!

Within a couple of months The Champ had emerged, fully-fledged By this time he had fought and beaten every dog I knew of in the district.

And we *didn't* approve! What we had wanted was a dog who could stand up for himself, if necessary. What we had got was an indefatigable Cassius Clay of a dog, who won't miss an opportunity of proving that he's the greatest!

BEFORE The Champ can be let to run free, I have to get to a really good vantage point and scan the surrounding countryside thoroughly for any "enemies."

The sound or the sight of another hound, big or small, and The Champ has to wait for his freedom. Otherwise, as I know to my cost, he'd be off, all five stone of him hurtling through space, as though he were a greyhound, my frantic commands following unavailingly in his wake.

Why do I put up with it?

The truth is, that though he's The Champ out-of-doors, indoors he's still our "Lucky-Puppy." His favourite seat is still a lap, though nowadays three-quarters of him hangs off the largest of laps.

He greets us individually each morning, as though he hadn't seen us for a year, and it never fails to warm us. He plays the clown in all sorts of ways, from appearing encased in a cardboard carton with only his feet visible, to running off with a cascading garden sprinkler and soaking all-comers.

Yes, indoors he is soft and playful and unshakably loyal.

Just mention the magic word "walk," however.

Then it's you and The Champ against the world. And The Champ (unfortunately for you) means to win. Every time! ∎

Continued from page 66

jected to examination or sometimes operations. Many scientists, physicists and astronomers still refuse to take UFOs seriously as a physical fact, and all kinds of theories have been put forward about the reality of these "abductions." Are they some kind of fantasy which the participants sincerely believe to be true, or were they real?

Either way, abduction reports from Brazil in recent years seem alarmingly true. There have been sightings of UFOs by hundreds of people at a time, and the glow of their lights has hurt witnesses' eyes and caused sickness. People have been relentlessly pursued by small craft which shine a beam of light on their victim to try to draw them

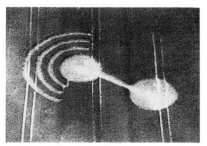

up into the machine.

There are stories of people clinging to trees to resist capture, or hanging suspended in the air before being returned to the ground.

Some are left with burned skin, numbness, sickness and headaches, and those who say they actually entered the craft are found days later in very poor condition, with little recollection of what happened after their encounter with the UFOs' small occupants.

Some have lost hair and teeth, or have what appear to be injection marks, some are temporarily speechless, and all are shocked and badly affected by their experience. In some areas, people are afraid to go out at night because of the UFOs.

Back in Britain, the latest unexplained mystery, Crop Circles, has been linked with UFOs by people who believe that as the circles become larger and more complex in design every year, there must be an intelligence behind the phenomenon. Are they trying to tell us something?

Apparently, at one of his conferences with Mikhail Gorbachev, President Bush said that if the earth were invaded by extraterrestrials, the United States and Soviet Union would join forces to repel them, but Gorbachev thought it too early to worry about such a possibility.

I hope he is right! ■

In June 1990, weird new patterns appeared in cereal fields in Hampshire. (Above, top and below.)

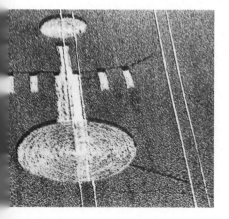

TAKE TWO

... put them in an old, battered car, add one persistent Frenchman, and you've got a holiday none of them is ever likely to forget!

GIRLS

Complete Story by
SUSAN SALLIS

A S she wrestled with the unfamiliar gear stick for the umpteenth time, Gillian Peters risked a quick sideways glance at her friend's profile. Gillian saw exactly what she expected.

Diana continued to gaze with a bored expression at the long, dusty road ahead, totally unconcerned that the car they had hired at Dieppe would never get them to Rouen, let alone Paris . . . Orleans . . . Limoges . . . Bordeaux and Spain.

Gillian sighed, remembering how she'd spent the winter planning the route to take in cathedrals, vineyards, the pines and lagoons of Les Landes and the Pyrenees. That was the only thing that had made the winter bearable.

And now it was all going wrong, right at the beginning — ever since Diana had got an address from a boyfriend of a garage where self-drive cars were so cheap that it wouldn't pay them to take Gillian's old banger over on the ferry.

Gillian scraped the gears again. No wonder they didn't charge much, she thought grimly. She looked at her friend and realised that would help considerably if Diana didn't look quite so fed-up.

Their eyes met and Diana brushed back her long hair with one hand while she turned in her seat.

"Can't we go any faster, Gilly?" she almost pleaded. "It was you who wanted to see Rouen Cathedral in the evening light."

"And it was you who wanted to hire this . . . this old crate!" Gillian replied shortly. "The accelerator's nearly through the floor as is!"

71

Diana subsided sulkily and again her hair streamed out behind her.

With an inward sigh of resignation, Gillian realised that cathedrals and quiet vineyards would be rather a waste on Diana. Yes, she would have been happier with the jet-set in Cannes or Nice, or the social whirl of Paris. In fact, Gillian couldn't understand why Diana had been so keen to come in the first place.

Gillian had been in the typing pool, telling Sally Mason about the proposed trip, when Diana had joined them.

"Orleans, did you say?" Diana had asked, unusually interested. She was in the Public Relations Department, usually far above mere typists.

"Then across the high land and down into Limoges," Gillian had added, swept on by the impetus of her own enthusiasm.

"There are vineyards all around Orleans, aren't there?" Diana had asked. "I believe you can visit some of them."

"Oh, yes." Gillian had beamed at her new audience. "I'm staying at one of them, as a matter of fact."

"How on earth can you afford this trip?" Diana sat herself on the corner of Sally's desk, obviously intending to stay.

"Well, I've had to save for a couple of years, of course. And I'll have to cut out all extras — no fancy meals and so on. I'm taking the car and I'll buy cheese and fruit and picnic as I go along."

"What a wonderful idea." Diana had gazed at her speculatively. "Of course, if you took someone with you it would halve the cost, wouldn't it?"

Gillian had laughed. "People want beaches — night clubs. No-one's interested in the kind of things I like."

Then, to Gillian's and Sally's amazement, Diana had said, "I'd love to come — if you'll have me."

SO here we are, Gillian thought miserably, right at the beginning of the trip, and Diana bored already.

She hadn't wanted to see the famous war-time beaches, or shop for a picnic in the market, and she wasn't in the least interested that Gillian was having such a job with the ancient car.

It looked like being a long, hard haul.

With another inward sigh, Gillian indicated left and began to pull out to overtake a lorry doing all of 25 miles an hour.

As she did so, a red sports car appeared in her mirror, a tiny dot in the empty distance behind her.

She was only just settling back into place in front of the lorry when it became life-size and flashed past them.

"Phew!" Diana sat up straight in admiration. "He must have been doing eighty at least."

"Or she," Gillian murmured.

"It was a he. Surely you noticed him? He was very dark — sort of went with the car."

"At that speed I don't see how you could possibly tell —"

"As a matter of fact, he waved. He noticed us, all right."

"Oh." Gillian didn't like the sound of the driver of the red sports car.

Men who drove cars like that and waved at girls they didn't know were the kind her mother had warned her against.

"Very Latin," Diana went on. "And he must be rich to have a car like that."

"Yes." Unaccountably, ridiculously, Gillian felt nervous. "Heading straight for Paris and the bright lights, I suppose."

Diana slumped again. "Oh, yes. Rouen's first on your list." She paused. "Gilly, I suppose you're absolutely set on seeing that old Cathedral?"

"At sunset," Gillian agreed somewhat grimly.

However, when they finally arrived, even Diana had to smile at the welcome they received — the "English tea" served in the panelled dining-room, the leisurely selection from the menu.

But at Gillian's suggestion of looking at the Cathedral she balked.

"You go along, Gilly," she insisted. "You know you'll enjoy it better without me. And I *would* like to see some of the shops."

So Gillian found herself entering the dim peace of a huge Cathedral nave alone.

She bought a traditional candle, walked through the wide bars of coloured light that splashed on the old stone floor from the famous windows.

She explored the chapels and sat in the nave absorbing the atmosphere of the place.

Then after 10 minutes — 10 very enjoyable minutes — she had that odd, indefinable feeling of being watched.

The lights had not yet been lit and it was growing dark in the huge nave. Somewhere near at hand, Vespers were being sung and the smell of incense was in the air.

She told herself it was her imagination. She stood up, casually took her time about gathering up her handbag and camera and turned round.

There was a scattering of elderly, black-clad ladies, some American couples — and lounging against an enormous stone pillar a very dark man, typically Latin, with a warm, olive skin and humorous eyes.

Gillian let her gaze travel on up into the ceiling. Then very normally she shouldered her bag and camera and moved down the aisle to the door.

It was much too dark for anyone to notice her warm face, and once outside in the golden evening her fast walk could be . . . well, simply to catch a bus.

THE next morning the sun shone warmly as the two girls climbed into the car and waved their farewells to the friendly hotelier.

However, they had gone only about 15 kilometres when the red dot appeared in the driving mirror.

Gillian pushed the accelerator farther into the floor.

"Bravo!" Diana called as she wound her window right down and let the wind take her hair. "I thought you were being a bit cautious. Getting used to driving on the right-hand side now?"

"I expect so," Gillian said, willing the car to go faster.

Even so, the sports car materialised with frightening rapidity in the mirror and swept past them a few moments later.

Its driver waved a gay salute and Gillian just had time to notice humorous, brown eyes and warm, olive face before the car disappeared.

"I hope you saw him that time!" Diana gasped.

"I did. Showing off, of course."

"He must have stayed in Rouen overnight."

"He was in the Cathedral last night, so I suppose he must have."

"In the Cathedral!" Diana shouted. "You didn't tell me! How did you know?"

"I didn't. Then."

"Oh, Gilly — honestly! Did he speak to you?"

"No. Probably it was you he was looking for. I got out fast," Gillian said.

"To think I was window-shopping," Diana mourned. "Still, there's hope yet. Gilly, can't you make this thing go faster?"

"Don't be silly, Diana," Gillian said with satisfaction. "We don't stand a chance of catching up with that car."

Nevertheless they passed the sports car standing in the forecourt of a filling-station.

"Yippee!" Diana said.

Gillian's one satisfaction was that there had been no sign of the driver so, presumably, he wouldn't know they'd gone past and might well wait some time. That was . . . if he was . . . well, interested in them.

Sure enough, it was an hour later when the red car overtook them again.

This time Diana was ready and went on waving until it vanished round the next bend.

"He'll be watching in his rear-view mirror," she said confidently.

"I wish you wouldn't, Diana," Gillian said uncomfortably. "We might have a job getting rid of him —"

"Who wants to get rid of him?" Diana cut in, genuinely astonished. "He's obviously very well off, and we don't really *have* to stick to your wretched itinerary."

"Diana, you know I've been planning this trip for ages."

"All right, keep calm. But if he *was* going our way, there'd be no harm in his showing us around Paris, would there?"

"Diana, we couldn't afford the sort of places he'd be used to! And we couldn't accept —"

"Who couldn't? What you really mean, Gilly, is that *you* wouldn't want to go to the sort of places he can afford! You want to do the usual dreary tourist round, Notre Dame, the Louvre —"

"Look, Gilly, there he is again. At that roadside café. Stop. We can do with some coffee and it's the perfect excuse!"

If your child must spend a little time in hospital, a few of his own familiar toys will be a great comfort.

thelwell's
BRAT RACE
CHILDREN'S WARD

Some children are a little suspicious of medical examination.

Many children adapt quickly to their new situation.

Treatment should be made as much fun as possible.

The day he comes out.

Highly-trained specialists are quick to diagnose the cause of the trouble.

Gillian didn't answer but her foot stayed firmly on the accelerator and they swept past the café and took the right fork signposted: *Orleans. Two Hundred Kilometres.*

"You've taken the wrong road, Gilly," Diana said frantically. "Paris was to the left!"

"I know. We can go to Paris on our way back."

"Our reservation —"

Gillian sighed. "Oh, all right. I've only got to take the next on the left. Stop worrying."

"But we've lost him," Diana said, mournfully. "He saw us take the Orleans road. He'll go on to Paris — alone."

Gillian allowed herself a small smile. So he would, she thought. She didn't care if she was a bit of a prig, a typical tourist, a non-adventuress. After all, it was originally her trip.

D IANA still wasn't speaking when they drew up at the next small café on a terrace overlooking the flat countryside.

Gillian parked the car next to the petrol pumps in the forecourt and led the way up the stairs. Diana followed ungraciously.

"I do think you're . . . unenterprising, Gilly," she said. "Most people come abroad to meet the people — as well as see the sights."

"Be honest, Diana. Would you be interested in that man if he wasn't so obviously rich?"

Diana gave a rueful smile.

"Perhaps not," she said with engaging honesty. "It's a strange thing — I'm often attracted to men with money."

She looked roguishly at Gillian and at last they both laughed together.

And just at that moment the red car cruised by, the dark man stared up through dark glasses, saw them, waved joyously and drove on at a reasonable pace.

"There!" Diana slapped the iron table triumphantly. "You see? He *is* interested. He just wants to get to know us — in the nicest possible way. He could have stopped — but no. He leaves it to us. He's going slowly enough for us to overtake him — if we want to."

"Oh, dear." Gillian sighed audibly this time, realising that she could no longer hold out against the attentions of their Latin . . . follower.

She left Diana to pay for the coffee and wandered down to the car. The smiling mechanic had the bonnet up and was checking the oil.

"She is very old, mademoiselle," he said with a shrug. "You have not far to go?"

"Les Landes — I hope," Gillian replied.

The mechanic looked at the engine, then turned away with a doubtful expression.

Suddenly Gillian had a brainwave. She reached into the engine and the next minute the rotor arm was in her handbag.

She walked across to pay the mechanic, thinking how far the sports car would be by now. She smiled to herself.

Diana came down the steps and settled herself in the passenger's seat.

"Let's go," she said, running her fingers through her long hair.

Gillian's smile froze. She felt ridiculously guilty as she climbed in beside Diana and switched on . . .

Five minutes later even Diana had to admit defeat. The mechanic didn't bother with more than a cursory glance beneath the bonnet.

"I will give a thorough inspection later, mademoiselle," he promised. "But the car is . . . er . . . how you say, worn out? Yes?"

"Yes," Gillian agreed, not meeting his eye.

She watched the old car being pushed into the garage and silently apologised to it.

Later — after lunch maybe — she would give it back its rotor arm and let it make a miraculous recovery, by which time the red sports car would be lost in the teeming millions of Paris.

She and Diana were sipping drinks on the terrace when a familiar engine purr sounded below them. They looked down, Gillian with horror and Diana with jubilation, at the familiar dark face smiling up at them.

"Damsels in distress, I understand?" he called in a delightful accent as he levered himself out of the driver's seat.

"May I intrude on your privacy for just long enough to make a suggestion?" He took the stairs two at a time.

"We have almost met several times before," Diana said coquettishly.

"Ah, but I would not have returned if I hadn't thought your car was . . . *malade*." He returned Diana's smile and then looked across the table at Gillian. "I am not welcome, mademoiselle?"

Gillian felt her face flame. "Of course, that is . . . I mean to say —"

She stopped and swallowed as Diana's lilting laugh cut across anything else she might say.

"You are more than welcome, monsieur. Our car, as you say, is *malade*. And we are stranded here with Paris just over the horizon —" It was amazing how lyrical Diana could sound.

He introduced himself. "I am Marc Riviere, and I am driving to Paris. If I may be of assistance, mademoiselle . . ."

Diana's glad cries could be heard for miles.

"And then I go on to Bordeaux. I am staying one night only in Paris, to visit relations."

Gillian sat upright. It all sounded so . . . normal, the sort of thing she herself might do. She let her eyes leave her glass for an instant.

He was staring at her as he had stared from the pillar in Rouen Cathedral. She dropped her gaze quickly.

"I'm Diana," Diana was saying. "And this is Gillian. And it's the strangest coincidence that ever could have happened — you'll never believe it. We're going to Bordeaux too. Aren't we, Gilly?" she finished challengingly.

"Well — yes," Gillian admitted reluctantly.

"I am not surprised. Not at all." He was still smiling, warmly, as if they weren't strangers at all but old friends who hadn't met for a long time. "You like the things I like. The off-beat tracks — yes? The Cathedrals — yes?"

Diana cleared her throat. "Oh. Yes. Certainly. And the excitement of Paris —"

"I have not been there—" he said.

Gillian looked up, startled, and met the warm, brown eyes fully. Yes, he was a man of the South.

"My sister is married and lives there and always she asks me to visit her," he went on. "So when my boss asks me to fetch his car from Dieppe, I ask him if I can use my holidays to see her and visit places I have never seen.

"And I pass two very English girls who are doing the same thing — yes?"

Diana was silent but Gillian said fervently, "Yes!"

Marc started to laugh.

"All this," he said and waved an airy hand at the old car below. "It is all . . . destiny. Yes?"

Gillian remembered the rotor arm in her handbag and went bright red.

He smiled. "To see the Louvre and Notre Dame in the company of someone so — *sympathique*. And then perhaps to take you south to my own country?"

"Look. I hate to be a spoil-sport," Diana said, "but could you possibly manage without me after Orleans?

"You see, I didn't want to mention this earlier, but there is someone there I rather want to look up. He owns one of the vineyards in that area, actually, and I did intend staying a few days anyway."

"Oh, Diana!" Gillian said reproachfully.

"Oh, stop fussing, Gilly! I'll be with you in Paris and you know you'd rather be alone, anyway. You can hire another car in Bordeaux and do all those drives along the dunes you were on about —"

"Perhaps I may take you, Miss Gilly? I spent a lot of time in Les Landes when I was a boy."

Gillian thought that Marc looked quite undismayed at losing Diana. Then through her utter confusion she remembered that Diana's enthusiasm for the trip dated from the moment she realised it included Orleans and the vineyards.

She turned to Marc.

"We must see," she said primly. "There is a lot of arranging to do. And you have your job."

TWO days later, the red sports car pulled away from Orleans and started the long climb into the Massif Central.

Already Gillian felt she had known Marc for years. His

enthusiasm during the long walks around the tourist sights of Paris had equalled her own. And his sister had been so friendly — so ordinary — so kind.

Even Diana had enjoyed it, though she had been more than ready for what she called "a touch of the luxuries" when she telephoned her vineyard owner from Orleans.

"We'll go and collect the car from that garage," she'd promised Gillian. "It'll be here when you get back. Enjoy yourself. Who ever would have thought he was your type!"

"We're just friends," Gillian protested.

Diana rolled her eyes. "Where have I heard that before?" she asked rhetorically. "A trip to the Spanish border in a car like that . . . and it just happened!"

Gillian wondered what she would say when the mechanic outside Rouen reported a missing rotor arm . . .

Meanwhile she and Marc were on their way to the high lands and the car was taking the gradient in a way the old hired car never could.

Gillian mentioned as much and was surprised when Marc started to laugh.

"You would have got her up here!" he assured her. "It was the way you coaxed that car along the road that made me feel we were — how do you say it?"

"Two of a kind?" she suggested with her eyes firmly on the road ahead.

"All right. Two of a kind. My job is with engines. And you have a feeling for them. Yes?"

There was something in his voice that made her face begin to feel warm again.

"I do my own servicing, if that's what you mean," she said stiffly.

"*Bien!* Good. And your own — how can we put it — your own de-servicing perhaps?" He picked up her handbag and weighed it judiciously in one hand.

"You know!" she accused him.

"I happened to see a rotor arm in your handbag yesterday. Yes."

"Marc, you don't understand. I thought if the car was out of action you would go on — even Diana said as much —"

"Oh yes, little Gilly. I understand this. Only too well." He smiled sideways at her, a little sadly. "Did I frighten you so much, *ma petite?* In the Cathedral perhaps? I was enjoying seeing you enjoying yourself."

"I wasn't frightened of *you,* Marc."

"Then of whom, Gilly?"

"I think — I think —" Gillian's face was very red. "I think that perhaps — I was afraid of myself."

"Ah . . ." Marc sighed. "Then that is very wonderful, my little English mechanic."

——————— * **THE END** * ———————

I KNEW my mother would hate the dress in the boutique, but it was exactly what I wanted for the youth club's summer disco. So I persuaded her to come and have a look at it, and hoped for a miracle.

Mum's a pet, but not very "with it" when it comes to clothes. It even took me ages to persuade her to let me wear jeans.

"They're workmen's clothes, Cath. Fine if you're a mechanic in a garage, but not if you're a pretty, dainty sixteen-year-old."

I don't want to be pretty and dainty. I want to be striking and stunning like my friend, Amber Mayhew, who's a year older than I am. Amber's got green eyes and thick, dark hair, lovely and straight and heavy it is. And she can do anything with it. Let it hang down below her shoulders, tie it back or pile it up high on top.

Mine's light brown, very fine, and it goes its own way no matter what I do with it. Mum says it suits my delicate features. That's another phrase that makes me curl up inside!

Anyway, Mum took one look at the dress in the boutique window and said, "Hideous!" just like I knew she would.

What was wrong with it, I asked and wished I hadn't because the answer was "everything" apparently.

Standing with her head slightly tilted in front of the shop window, Mum stabbed her finger at the pane.

"Just look at the colours — " she said, turning away from it as if in pain.

I stuck my neck out again. "What's wrong with them?"

"Charcoal grey." She moaned. "Muddy brown and magenta. Those horrible streaks of magenta!" Mum shook her head in desperation.

"Did you know there was a battle of Magenta and that's where the colour's supposed to have got its name?" I asked brightly, grabbing at the opportunity to divert her a little.

Ignoring this snippet of information, she brought her gaze back to the dress.

"And there's absolutely no shape in it," she observed. "In fact, it's straight up and down like a yard of pump water, as my old gran used to say."

"The idea is you put some shape into it by wearing it," I explained patiently.

Mum gave a contemptuous snort. "Mae West couldn't put shape into that thing!"

"If I were to try it on, let you see me in it," I suggested. "It might grow on you, Mum."

"Heaven forbid," she muttered.

I seemed to have run out of arguments.

"What did you have in mind, then?" I inquired, needing time to reassemble my shattered forces of persuasion.

Mum thought it over.

"White, with a pretty little flower in pink or blue. Narrow-waisted,

THE NEXT GENERATION

Mums — there's one thing you should remember when dealing with your teenage daughter. And that's how you used to be yourself . . .

Complete Story by STELLA BLAINEY

full-skirted, organdie, tulle and swiss voile."

She carolled the words, her eyes shining as she visualised the dress of her dreams.

"Mum!" I shrieked. "I'm sixteen, not six!"

My mother opened her eyes and came down to earth.

"I know how old you are, Cathy, *and* I know what suits you. And if you think I'd let you go to this youth club thing wearing that . . . that . . ."

"It's a disco dance, not a garden party. Pop records and . . . anything goes," I said.

And then I gave up. "I knew you wouldn't like it. We may as well go home."

We turned and began the 10-minute walk back in silence.

WHY had I asked Mum to come and see the dress? I must have been mad even to mention it.

Hoping for a miracle? You're nuts! I told myself. As for that stupid little lump in your throat — you're being ridiculous. You know perfectly well it was useless even to hope of getting that dress.

I'd wear my jeans to the dance, with a dark blouse and lots of beads, I decided.

Brian Conlan liked me in jeans. He'd said so the first time I wore them to the youth club.

I had a quick, mental picture of Brian. His hair, springing back from his forehead, thick and brown, the colour of the acorns we picked up in the park sometimes. His eyes, sometimes they looked grey and other times green. They twinkled when he smiled.

Brian. Just thinking about him made me go all queasy inside, the same way you feel when you're going up the slope on a roller coaster. But in a nice kind of way.

Brian. How I wished he could have seen me in that dress.

Lucky Amber Mayhew, I thought. She can wear what she likes, do what she likes.

Deep down inside me, though, I didn't really envy her. She was allowed to do pretty much what she wanted because her parents were separated, and neither of them seemed to care what Amber did. Maybe that's why she came to our house so often, and sat around while I played my guitar.

My mother made a fuss of Amber and Dad teased her. Amber thought the world of both of them.

Amber had lots of pocket money and a clothing allowance but her parents weren't interested in what she did with it.

"What's Amber going to wear to the dance?" Mum's voice cut in on my thoughts, just as though she'd read them.

"She's got a new dress. A sort of pea-soup colour with bands of faded purple. It's freaky, Mum, really freaky!"

My mother shuddered. "It certainly sounds like it."

"You don't understand, Mum. Freaky means it turns us on. We really go for it. We like it."

"Chic, that's what we used to call a smart outfit when I was your age."

"Sheik?" I was visualising an Arab chieftain in a long, flowing robe.

"C-h-i-c." She spelt it out for me. "Chic. It means neat, smart, sophisticated. I remember an outfit I had once . . ."

Mum went off into a dream, while I thought what funny words they had then.

We were halfway home when she stopped walking suddenly, and started nibbling the tip of her right index finger. It's a thing Mum does when she's thinking hard, and it sets my teeth on edge.

So I stood and looked into the butcher's window while I waited for her to catch up with me.

I was counting a tray of sausages for the second time when she grabbed me by the arm and spun me round.

"I haven't been fair to you, Cath," she said. "Come on."

I WAS so surprised, I just stood there gaping until she gave me a gentle tug.

"Come on. Someone else might be after it, though I doubt it." She smiled, walking rapidly.

As I broke into a half-run trying to keep up with her, she explained her change of mind "I was remembering my black outfit . . ."

"Your black outfit?" I was puffing now.

"Yes. I was fifteen and I'd never been allowed to wear black. But I'd seen a beautiful black coat, close fitting, with long, tight sleeves. I pestered the life out of my poor mother to let me have it. And in the end she did. But much against her will.

"I made myself a little black velvet cap to go with it. Juliet caps, we used to call them. And it had a tiny veil that came halfway down my forehead. I had black, patent, leather court shoes with very high, slim heels, and black gloves and bag."

"*Everything* black?" I queried, breaking into a near gallop as Mum stepped up her pace still further. She nodded.

"Oh, how I loved that outfit, in spite of what old Mrs Mason said."

"Who was old Mrs Mason?"

"An old lady who lived near us," Mum said. "I was wearing my black outfit for the first time to go to Sunday morning service. Showing it off, I felt madly smart and . . ."

"Chic?" I suggested.

"Yes. Then old Mrs Mason popped out of her house as I was passing and said, 'Oh, you poor child, you've suffered a bereavement. Not one of your parents, I hope?' I was furious with her."

Mum laughed. Then she said quietly, "My mother felt exactly the same way about that coat as I do about this dress you're so keen on, but she let me have it. So, I hope you'll enjoy wearing the dress, Cath." *Continued on page 87*

A ONE, TWO, THREE, FOUR-LEGGED FIEND!

Lucky horseshoes for the happy couple . . . We got four of them, says Mervyn Watkins. The only trouble was they were still occupied!

MY fiancée and I both came from large families, so it was inevitable that our wedding day was like a meeting of the clans. After a very boisterous reception, Jan and I were relieved to slip away for a quiet, peaceful honeymoon. We drove off to our little haven in the Welsh hills.

My uncle had lent us his white-washed cottage for the honeymoon.

It was part of a rambling old farm, boasting a few chickens, cows and sheep, but no other inhabitants — apart from the inevitable mountain ponies!

All we had to do was keep an eye on the livestock. Otherwise we could just please ourselves.

The cottage looked as though it had grown naturally out of the mountain. In fact, the roof of the privy was overgrown with grass, just an extension of the mountain itself, and Uncle had warned us that sheep often stood on the privy roof while grazing.

After we'd unpacked and explored the cottage, we stood hand-in-hand watching the setting sun. Then, we said goodnight to the idyllic summer evening, shooed a stray sheep off the privy roof, and went off to bed.

★ ★ ★ ★

In the middle of the night I awoke with a start. My new bride was vigorously shaking my shoulder.

"Mervyn!" she said in choked alarm. "There's someone in the cottage!"

I sat up with a start and listened. Sure enough, someone was clumping around the other end of the cottage.

The clumping continued as I tried to light the oil lamp, my hands shaking.

At last I had it lit. I crept out of bed and reached for my dressing-gown and slippers.

"You stay under the bedclothes!" I instructed my bride.

But she was determined not to be left alone.

The clumping was very persistent by now and seemed to be getting louder.

"Oh, Mervyn!" Jan wailed through her chattering teeth.

By
MERVYN
WATKINS

"Maybe we should have stayed at a hotel . . ."

Resolutely I took her hand and holding the lamp high, I led the way. I would start my married life the way I meant to go on!

WARILY I opened the door and peered into the living-room. The lamp cast an eerie halo of light about the place.

We opened the living-room door and peered into the kitchen. Nothing!

"So far, so good," I remarked bravely.

But Jan wasn't amused. She peered wide-eyed over my shoulder as we heard the next thump.

This time I nearly dropped the lamp.

"It's . . . it's in the privy!" Jan said aghast.

This time there was a snort and a kind of heavy breathing, followed by a second snort and a sound like an animal pawing the ground.

"It's a pony, Jan!" I said with a sigh of relief. "It's a mountain pony standing on the privy roof!"

I saw her smile in the lamplight.

"Oh, how ridiculous!" she scolded herself. "And I thought . . ."

"I imagined all sorts of things, too," I said reassuringly.

We unlocked the kitchen door which adjoined the privy and looked up into the starry sky.

There, sure enough, its mane ruffled in silhouette, was a mountain pony standing on the privy roof.

"Shoo!" Jan tried to scare it, but the beast watched us curiously. I held the oil lamp high, hoping to dazzle and frighten it off, but it just bent its neck nearer to inspect us.

"It's a very tame pony," Jan remarked. "Maybe your uncle feeds it. Perhaps it's hungry now?"

In my book, the middle of the night was definitely not feeding time.

"Oi! Hop it!" I shouted sharply.

But the pony just looked down at us. I swear he was grinning at me, but maybe it was the lurid glow of the lamp.

"I saw a film once where these Indians besieged some white settlers in a hut," I remembered unhelpfully. "The Indians drove the local cattle on to the roof to make it cave in."

"What happened?" Jan asked.

85

"The settlers set fire to the roof and drove the cattle away."

"Oh!" she said in disappointment. "That doesn't really help us, does it?"

Then suddenly the pony solved the problem for us. It snorted and moved off the privy roof and disappeared on to the mountain with a parting whinny.

WE'D just settled down again when we were awakened a second time by a terrible crash. Automatically, I reached for the matches and battled with the lamp again.

Jan sat up, staring ahead in disbelief.

I was already halfway to the door and she sprang out of bed after me.

"At least we'll always be close," I joked as she grabbed my arm. "Calamity brings people together!"

This time we went straight to the source of the noise.

"It sounded like an earthquake . . ." Jan began, then froze as we entered the kitchen.

The cottage was suddenly filled with a loud neighing sound.

This time, as we unlocked the kitchen door, we heard a great snorting and stamping. But there was no pony on the privy roof.

"It's inside!" Jan yelled. "Mervyn it's *in* the privy!"

I didn't believe her, but it was true. The pony had come through the roof and was now stamping about inside.

I was all for retreating and waiting until daylight, but the maternal instinct in my wife won the day.

"Oh, Mervyn, it might be injured! Perhaps it's broken a leg, or something . . ."

"No, it's just stuck," I answered her. "Hold the lamp, Jan. We'll need more light."

I lit the lamp in the kitchen and lounge then rejoined Jan in the tiny backyard.

"Stand back," I warned her. "It may charge out."

Gingerly I gripped the handle of the privy door, gave a mighty push and stood back.

But no foam-flecked stallion charged out as I'd expected.

Just a gentle snort, a shuffle of hooves on the stone flags, then a curious face emerged.

It was the same pony all right. We could tell by the look in its eyes.

It may have suffered a shock to its pride, but no more. It shook itself and clopped outside on to the backyard.

"It's all right, Jan. It's tame," I ventured, and had a quick peep into the privy.

The floor was covered in earth and stones. Where the roof had been the stars now twinkled. The pony's weight had been too much for the privy roof.

"What are we going to do?" Jan prompted me, now that she knew the pony wasn't hurt.

As I turned to look at the high brick wall surrounding us, the pony moved closer and nudged its velvet muzzle against my chest.

"Whoa there, boy," I said, trying to repress my alarm. I wasn't used to animals.

"Oh, he's quite a dear, really," my wife said, warming to our surprise guest.

While she was drooling over our visitor, I was trying to work out how we could get rid of him.

"There's no way out for it," I concluded glumly. "The darned thing's stuck here! I think we should wait until daylight . . ."

"We'll just have to take him through the cottage," Jan decided.

"We can't coop him up here all night."

As if to confirm her plan of action, she passed me the lamp and slid her arms round the pony's neck.

"You lead the way, Mervyn," she instructed. "We'll follow on."

"But what about the inside of Uncle's cottage?" I protested weakly. "The beast's already wrecked the outside . . ."

So for the first time in my married life, I learned that it was useless trying to argue with a woman.

A very improbable scene it was, but that's how it happened, me tentatively leading the way, and my new bride escorting a shaggy, mud-encrusted mountain pony through the kitchen, into the living-room, through the hall and so out through the front door.

As I unlocked the front door to let our visitor out, I was convinced I was having a nightmare.

But as Jan coaxed the pony outside, it turned its head to face me in the lamplight. And with a final parting whinny it cantered away into the darkness.

"I swear it grinned at me!" I insisted, as my bride and I returned to bed.

We never saw that pony again, but it wasn't a phantom. The remainder of my honeymoon spent mending the privy roof was proof of that! ∎

Continued from page 83

"Oh, Mum. Thanks. Thanks." I squeezed her arm as we ran the last few yards to the shop.

★　　　★　　　★　　　★

We took it easy going home. I opened the yellow carrier bag for a quick peep at the dress while Mum popped into the butcher's for some chops. Amber was coming to have dinner with us and I was looking forward to showing her the dress.

I was just having a final peep before closing the bag when a voice said, "Cathy," over my shoulder.

I jumped and turned round.

It was Brian. He must have been to the swimming baths. His hair was damp and he was clutching a rolled-up towel.

"Wow!" he said, peering into the yellow bag. "That for the dance, Cathy?"

I nodded, my cheeks flushing and my heart thumping all over the place.

Mum came out of the shop then and I introduced Brian to her.

Brian said, "Hello," nice and politely, but added that he'd better go, as he was late for dinner.

"I'll see you next week at the dance, Cathy." He smiled. "Goodbye, Mrs Fuller. That's a terrific dress Cathy's got, isn't it?"

Mum hesitated for a moment, frowning, and I knew she didn't want to let me down, bless her. Then her brow cleared and she winked at me before answering Brian.

"It's freaky. Positively freaky!" she declared.

—————— * **THE END** * ——————

A crisis brought her here to be with the only man she had ever loved — her best friend's husband . . .

JOURNEY INTO

S HE had to go to him. Nothing in the world mattered but that — going to him before it was too late.

She picked up the two-day-old copy of the little country newspaper and looked, once again, for his name, as she had so often looked for it in all the years she had loved him.

David Harrison, headmaster of the High School, was rushed to hospital yesterday, following a sudden collapse. He is now awaiting

Complete Story by
ISOBEL STEWART

YESTERDAY

an operation following the report of a neurological surgeon.

There were other words, words that blurred now before her eyes.

Blinding headaches . . . brain tumour. Linda folded the Leymouth Dispatch, and put it down on the table. There are things I have to do, she told herself, forcing down her blind panic. I have to phone the office and say I won't be coming in. I have to pack a suitcase and lock up the flat.

Her boss was a reasonable man. When she said there was a family illness, he told her to stay off as long as she was needed. But even as she thanked him, she knew it would have made no difference whatever he had said.

She was going to David, and nothing and nobody was going to stop her.

She packed a small suitcase and went over her flat carefully before locking up and going down to her car. It was only when she was on the motorway heading south for Leymouth that she caught a glimpse of herself in the driving mirror.

Her eyes were dark and tense. The thought she had been trying to push away was suddenly there in the anguish on her face.

What if I am too late?

The report had said "yesterday," and the paper was two days old. Since then, David might have become worse.

Since then — she forced herself to give words to the thought — David might have died. That would be too much to bear.

She forced herself to concentrate on her driving, to read the names that had once been so familiar to her. She pulled off the motorway and on to the small country roads that led over the gentle hills towards the sea.

Ten miles out of Leymouth she stopped for petrol. As she drew away from the petrol pump she saw a telephone box. It was only then she realised she couldn't just drive up to the hospital and ask to see him.

She pulled in beside the workshop. As she dialled the hospital, she noticed that for the first time since she had read the newspaper report her hands were shaking.

"Leymouth Hospital, can I help you?"

The voice was cool and crisp. Its detachment helped her to regain her control.

"I wanted to inquire about a patient — David Harrison," she said. It was strange to say his name aloud after all these years.

"Mr Harrison is as well as can be expected."

There was a moment of soaring relief, but she had to find out more.

"Wait — please," she said unsteadily. "When are your visiting hours?"

"Three to four. But Mr Harrison isn't allowed any visitors apart from his wife."

There was a hint of reproof in the voice, and it drained the last of her courage away. It was all she could do to ask the one last thing she wanted to know.

"Is he — conscious?"

"Yes, Mr Harrison is conscious. Who shall I say inquired?"

Clare hesitated.

"It — it doesn't matter," she said at last and put the receiver down.

She thought about the phone call as she drove the last 10 miles.

"AND I QUOTE . . ."

Mike Harding (1944-), was born and educated in Manchester. Despite holding an Education degree he has not taught, but he achieved success as an entertainer with songs and patter. He has written several books and plays, and is a keen rambler and cyclist.

◇ *The Do-It-Yourself fanatic's wife is usually a nervous wreck because everything in the house either falls on her, traps her, or gives her an electric shock.*

◇ *He was sent to prison for stealing an elastic band. Unfortunately the elastic band was wrapped around 80,000,000 francs.*

◇ *The first time I went to a posh kid's house, I couldn't understand why his eiderdown didn't have pockets and sleeves.*

◇ *Map reading is incredibly easy and can be learnt in a couple of centuries by anyone with a first-class degree in Geography or a doctorate in Mathematics.*

◇ *God didn't drive Adam and Eve out of the Garden of Eden, the midges did.*

Somehow it had put things into focus for her — made her realise she needed time to think.

The outskirts of Leymouth were achingly familiar and, without conscious thought, she took the road that led to the beach.

The sky was cloudy and the sea grey and heavy. There was no-one else on the beach. Her feet sank into the soft sand and she took her shoes off and carried them in her hand as she walked.

She was right to have come here, to the place where she had always brought her problems — to where she had always come when she needed to think.

Only his wife, only Margy, is allowed to visit David, the hospital had said.

But he is conscious, she thought. All I have to do is let him know I'm here and he'll tell them to let me in.

It doesn't even have to be a message, she thought, remembering

Continued on page 94

91

ALL THINGS DRIED

THIS is the time to give a little thought to those lovely indoor arrangements that can brighten your winter. So, late summer and autumn is the time to get in a good supply of material. It's only too easy to cut off every fading flower in a mad fit of tidying and regret it later on!

Take a look around the garden and make a note of those flowers you want to leave undisturbed until

The soft tones of dried grasses and seedheads can be highlighted with brightly-coloured dyed materials.

their seed pods have ripened. Decide which flowers you want to dry for their blooms, and cut a few stems as they flower. You can then hang them to dry until required.

Apart from the classic everlasting flowers like Helichrysum, Statice and Rhodanthe, all kinds of plants grown in the herbaceous border are useful.

Achillea is splendid, with its great, flat, yellow flowers which dry a tawny colour, and they mix well with branched sprays of steely-blue Sea Holly (Eryngium), all spikes and ruffs.

Stalks of the curious Acanthus flowers dry to a pleasant, soft blend of mauve and grey, and make a lovely centrepiece for a large vase. Echinops are valuable for their globe-shaped thistle heads, and a feathery cloud of Gypsophila gives a softening effect overall. Cut this one with really long stems.

Delphiniums are good, too, but try using the side shoots of the dark blue varieties. The lighter colours are a bit insipid when dried. And don't forget the long bell-ropes of love-lies-bleeding (Amaranthus) — they can provide some graceful downward curves.

If possible, do dry a few stems of Stachys lanata. Its fat, woolly stems wreathed with purplish pink flowers make a charming picture of mauve and silver. You don't grow it?

You can soon put that right! It's a good, easy herbaceous plant, spreads quickly in any reasonable soil and is commonly known as Lamb's Ear.

AND BEAUTIFUL

There's no need to buy expensive cut flowers to brighten your home on dark winter days, says Florence Bastie, for a little forethought will reward you with a wonderful store of Nature's treasures.

By FLORENCE BASTIE

This dainty basket forms an ideal container for an assortment of preserved garden flowers.

DRYING your chosen flowers is no problem. All it entails is stripping off the leaves, tying the stems into small bundles and hanging them in a dry place out of the sun. Strong sunlight bleaches the blooms. An airy shed is a good place, but not a greenhouse.

Indoors, a spare room is better than the kitchen, as this can get steamy.

Gather the flowers just before they open fully and hang them up until the stems are hard. Flowering grasses can be dried in the same way.

Some flowers will dry naturally if left standing in water in a warm room until the water has evaporated — this method is successful with hydrangeas. Cut these flowers when fully developed but not faded, hammer the ends of the stems and place in deep water immediately.

You can add variety to an arrangement with seed heads from various plants. Annual poppies have prettily-crowned pods which stay blue-green if cut as soon as the petals fall. Honesty (Lunaria) stays at its pearliest if gathered before it sheds its outer coat.

Since it is a biennial and dies after flowering, you can pull up whole plants and hang them upside down until quite dry, when the outer skins can be peeled away, to expose the "moons" within.

The little flat seeds are tucked between the inner and outer layers; remember to scatter a few of them for flowers another year.

I HAVE had a lot of fun trying unlikely plants. One year I let some love-in-the-mist (Nigella) form pods and they turned into filigree balloons — really beautiful and so delicate. They do really need to be picked when they reach the pod stage, however, as rain damages them.

The dusky cone centre of Rudbeckia, left after the petals have fallen, is another bonus.

Ornamental gourds are easy and fun to grow for their bright colours and queer shapes, and a bowl filled with them always makes an attractive conversation piece.

Remember to leave them until the short stem at the end of the gourd is quite hard before you pick them, or they will rot.

Even if you are unable to dry flowers, there are always leaves. The best method to preserve them is with glycerine and water. Make sure you gather your beech leaves early if you want that rich copper colour.

Split each stem up about an inch. Mix two parts hot water to one part glycerine and stand the stems in two to three inches of liquid.

After about a couple of weeks the leaves will take on a glossy look — this means they have absorbed the glycerine. Remove them from the liquid then, for if left too long they will become greasy.

Although beech is the best known, leaves from other shrubs and trees can be preserved as well. Maple, oak and hawthorn can all be treated. Magnolia leaves are particularly lovely, turning a bright, rich brown.

The important thing is to keep a look-out for interesting flowers and leaves, which because of their texture, colour or shape have real decorative value. Then experiment with them and build up a treasure store for the winter. ■

Continued from page 91

how they had parted. All I need to do is to ask the nurse to say to him, "Clare is here." It's as simple as that.

But was it simple? Was anything simple between her and David? Keeping apart for all these years certainly hadn't been.

If she did what her heart wanted her to do, what every bone in her body urged her to do, then Margy would find out, and there would be an end to the concealment of their love.

I have no right to see him. The thought struck her like a physical blow.

She sat down near the ruins of the old pier, where she and David had come that day so long ago. As she looked at the waves crashing into foam on the sand, today became yesterday, and she was back again when it all began.

★   ★   ★   ★

She had been born in Leymouth, and she had lived here until she was 19. It was then she went off to secretarial college in London. The city was noisy and bustling and exciting, but Clare knew that it wasn't the place for her.

She missed Leymouth too much, missed the quiet seaside town, the long beaches, the smell and the sound of the sea. She missed, too, her own family and friends, especially her closest friend, Margy.

Margy, whose excited letters had told her of the young school-teacher she had grown to love in the year Clare had been away.

I'm longing for you to meet David, she had written.

And later — *I'm so disappointed you won't be home for the wedding, Linda, but your job in Paris is such a super chance.*

It *was* a wonderful chance, and Clare had loved her year in Paris. But at the end, when she'd had to choose between staying on, or going home, there had been no doubt at all what she wanted to do.

She'd gone home to Leymouth, home to the sea and the sand, to her parents, to Margy, happily married and the mother of a baby boy with his father's grey eyes and his mother's fair curls.

And she'd met David.

SOMETIMES, in the years after she left Leymouth, she thought that it might have been easier for David and for her, if they had known in that first moment of meeting, if there had been an instant recognition of what they were to mean to each other. If there had been that flash of knowledge, she would have gone away there and then, running away from a danger she could not allow herself to face.

But there was nothing like that, for her or for him. He was simply her best friend's husband. At the start there was a cautious liking, a guarded friendship that perhaps blinded Clare to the possibility of anything else.

She and Margy had been close friends from the time they started school together, and it was a joy and a relief to both of them to find that neither Clare's time away from Leymouth nor Margy's marriage to David had made any difference to their friendship.

Naturally there were new areas of privacy, of reticence. For Margy, her relationship with her husband was something between the two of them, and the close exchange of confidences of their growing-up years was no longer possible.

Clare, too, found that there were parts of her own life, problems she came up against, that she had to work out for herself, that she preferred not to talk over with Margy.

Continued on page 98

CHILDREN are great fun to have around — for short periods of time.

However, after having them around uninterruptedly during the school holidays, I used to develop a disease called "The Togetherness Itch." The symptoms were an overpowering desire to lock the children in a cupboard until school started again, plus the urge to run away from home!

Anything there you recognise?

By RONI BORDEN

Well, I say "I used to," for though I know that, unfortunately, I can't cancel school holidays, I have come up with the next best thing. The cure for "The Itch."

The basis for the cure is adequate preparation. And, to be effective, the preparations should begin at least a month before the holiday is due to start.

I always start by praying with as much concentration as I can muster that the weather will stay fine throughout the week, fortnight, or whatever the period.

However, I'm fully aware that God helps those who help themselves, so I take additional important steps . . .

For a start, before the holidays begin, I buy what I consider to be at least a

HOW TO SURVIVE THE SCHOOL HOLIDAYS
— And Remain Sane!

All right, so you won't remain sane, says Roni Borden. But let's hope, with some of her "devious tricks," you might just survive!

month's supply of snacks. I have learned that, with care, a month's supply for adults can generally tide a teenager over for almost a week.

And I make certain that none of the food is perishable, so I can hide it away all over the house until the actual start of the holidays. I know that if I bring the whole lot out at once, everything will disappear the same day.

These snacks are useful in keeping the arguments down. Let me give you a couple of examples.

"Mum, she took my comic and didn't even ask permission!"

"That's OK. It'll give you a chance to find some chocolate biscuits before your sister gets them, and gobbles them up!"

"Mum! Dick's saxophone is making so much noise I can't even think!"

"Well, if you eat some potato crisps you can drown it out!"

And besides, children full of food are too lethargic to argue back.

THE next step is to check the news-papers the day before the holidays start and to memorise the names of all the suitable films and the cinemas that are showing them.

As far as I'm concerned, any film within a 30-mile radius of my home is worth considering — because any distance is worth driving if I can be guaranteed three peaceful hours! And when I can arrange to sit several rows away from the kids, I even get to enjoy the film.

During the week prior to the holidays I also make casual phone calls to the mothers of my children's friends. The conversation goes something a bit like this . . .

"Hello, Ann? I was wondering if you would like to go shopping one day next week. I need a new dress and I really would like a second opinion."

"Well, I'd love to. The only trouble is that it's the school holidays next week, and we'll have to drag the kids along."

"Oh, I forgot about that. We'll have to make it the week after next."

That lets me know for sure that Ann and her family are planning to be home during the week's holiday, and, if my son wants to spend a part of his holiday at a friend's house, I know exactly who to suggest.

Of course, I may have to go shopping one afternoon with Ann after school starts, but I probably would have gone shopping eventually, anyway.

It's also essential to a mother who wants some peace and quiet during school holidays that she remains absolutely unfamiliar with any of the games that the children own.

Thus, I can respond honestly to their requests:

"Mum, we need three people to play this game. Can you join in?"

"Oh," I say, staring at the box, "is that the game where you hide the little plastic things all over the house?"

"Never mind, Mum."

A short trip to the chemist is the final act of preparation — for ear-plugs and aspirin!

Being prepared is only 75 per cent. of the cure to "The Togetherness Itch."

Now, the mother who is looking for the 100 per cent. protection must also have some "specific moves" planned for the week or weeks in question . . .

FIRST, I always shorten the actual holiday by a day or two with a firm announcement on the first morning:

"Before you children do anything during this holiday you must tidy up your rooms."

Children do not submit lightly to such an order.

"Our rooms may look messy to you," they declare, "but we know just were everything is. It would be a disaster to make us change things around."

"The disaster would be if a fire started under that pile of junk. It would take two days before we even knew that anything was burning!" I answer.

And so the holidays begin . . .

I don't know if you've noticed it, but children who have difficulty in getting up in time for school never have this bother on holiday mornings. In fact, for some strange reason, children on holiday are able to wake up as much as an hour earlier than they would normally need to.

I have a plan to beat this, though. All I do is sneak into their rooms after they're asleep and put their clocks back an hour. Thus, in the morning, the children think they have woken up far too early and are in no rush to pop out of bed.

Unfortunately, this little trick only allows me extra sleep for one morning, because by the middle of the first day my kids have figured out that their clocks have a different time from the rest of the clocks in the house.

And if all this isn't enough, I have one private trick . . .

I keep a calendar under my bed, and at the end of each day I carefully cross out the day that has just passed. Then I know for certain that the days really are passing and that eventually the school holidays will come to an end! ■

Continued from page 95

But the warmth and the closeness were always there. Once when David was away on a course, and their young son, Timmy, had to be rushed to hospital with pneumonia, it was Clare who sat up all the long night with Margy. And when the dawn came and they knew that the little boy would be all right, it was Clare who held Margy while she wept her tears of exhaustion and relief.

And a year after that, when Clare's mother died, it was Margy who helped her to deal with the practical things that her father seemed unable to do, Margy who made her see beyond the shock and the loss, to the warmth and the love and the memories of her mother that would be with her for all the days of her life.

When David and Margy had a little girl, Veronica, soon after Timmy's second birthday, they asked Clare to be her godmother.

Clare held the baby at her christening, and when she saw David and Margy exchange a smile at the baby's outraged howl, there was a tightness in her throat.

She found herself hoping, not for the first time, that some day she would find the right man, the man she would love as Margy loved David, the man she would want to spend the rest of her life with.

There had been men, in those years she was back in Leymouth — men who were attracted to her red hair and her dark eyes, to her tall slimness, to the quiet warmth of her smile. Each time, she took the man she was interested in to meet Margy and David, and she knew that Margy, too, wondered each time if this was the one.

David said very little about the men in her life. He was a quiet man with rare flashes of humour. She knew that he was a popular teacher at the local High School.

But once, when Margy had asked her if she wanted to bring a man called Steve for supper again, and Clare told her that she wouldn't be seeing Steve again, David looked up from the exercise books he was correcting.

"I'm glad, Clare," he said, unexpectedly. "I didn't think he was really your type."

Clare looked at him, unable to hide her surprise, and he coloured.

"I found him just a bit too casual and light-hearted," he went on, slowly. "I shouldn't judge him after a few meetings, but I couldn't help feeling it wouldn't last. I hope you don't mind me saying so, but I've always felt you're too sensitive for his type."

"Well, yes," Clare agreed, somewhat abashed. "I know what you mean, and I agree. In time he'd have irritated me, and I'd probably have bored him."

When it is the right man, I'll know, she'd told herself more than once. It didn't really worry her that the years were slipping past, that she was 24. She enjoyed her work as receptionist to old Dr Clark, and she liked going home each night to the old stone house that had been her home all her life.

Sometimes Clare would tell herself that she should make a move, that she should be more ambitious, but there was a contentment about her life that satisfied her.

She had always loved the sea, and often in the evenings she would walk along the shore alone. And as she walked, she would think vaguely, uncertainly — some day, there will be someone. But there was no anxiety in the thought, only a feeling of waiting for the right man.

Then had come the day of the birthday party . . .

IT had been Margy's idea. Clare protested that she didn't want a party, but Margy said she needed one.

"And you're to wear that super blue caftan thing," she ordered.

"Why?" Clare asked her, smiling. "What's his name?"

"His name is Ken Johnson, and he's the new maths teacher,"

Continued on page 104

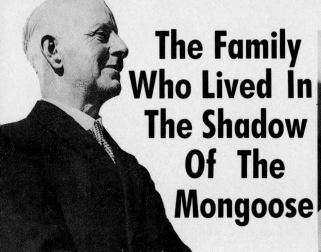

The Family Who Lived In The Shadow Of The Mongoose

One day in 1931, a strange visitor arrived at their Isle of Man home. He claimed to be eighty years old; his name, he said, was "Gef" — and he was a talking mongoose! His visit heralded a controversy which was to last for years — and the beginning of a truly baffling mystery!

THERE have been many mysteries in the realms of the supernatural that have defied rational explanation, but surely one of the most unusual ever was the strange case of Gef, the talking mongoose.

Late in the year of 1931, the national Press reported that a "man-weasel" which talked in a "piercing and uncanny voice" was haunting an isolated farmhouse on the Isle of Man.

It was the beginning of a mystery which was to endure down the years . . .

One evening in September 1931, life changed dramatically for the Irving family, in their farmhouse at Cashen's Gap. Mr James Irving heard a tapping noise in the attic, and thinking it might be rats or mice, he was about to investigate when the sound changed to barking and growling.

Then, more alarmingly, a loud crack shook the room, setting the pictures swinging. Irving went up to the attic. There was nothing to see, but the noises continued.

Experimentally, James Irving tried answering with bird and animal noises, repeating the name of the animal he was mimicking after each one. He was rather shaken when "back came the same sound and the human word for it in a shrill, high-pitched voice."

Soon, an incessant stream of chatter and questions from their invisible visitor tormented the Irvings. Night after night the strange little voice persisted.

"What in the name of God can

he be?" Irving whispered to his wife, but Gef, as he called himself, heard him and replied mockingly:

"I am a ghost in the form of a weasel, and I shall haunt you with weird noises and clanking chains."

Ghost or not, Irving decided to put down rat poison, but although Gef was heard to scream, apparently in agony, he was soon chattering as volubly as ever. But this time there was an implied threat.

"If you are kind to me, I will bring you good luck," he squeaked. "If you are not kind, I shall kill your poultry. I could kill you all if I liked, but I won't."

And just in case the Irvings cherished hopes that Gef might disappear as mysteriously as he came, their unseen companion told them:

"This is my house. It suits me."

It was easy to see why. When the Irvings first moved into their lonely farmhouse, they panelled the interior with matchboarding to keep out draughts, and the narrow cavity between the panelling and the original walls was now Gef's hideaway.

The Irvings never knew where he might be next. He seemed everywhere and nowhere, his shrill voice and mocking laugh joining in the conversation.

But whatever could he be? The Irvings knew that a local farmer had once brought Indian mongooses into the area to keep down the rabbits, but although Gef repudiated any relationship, he told them that he came from Delhi, and was born on June 7, 1852!

As Gef grew bolder, Mrs Irving and her 13-year-old daughter, Voirrey, sometimes glimpsed a little bushy tail disappearing through small holes in the wall. Once Voirrey got a better view and reported that Gef had a yellow face, rather like a hedgehog with a flattened snout.

Then one night the Irvings saw an animal's shadow cast by candlelight. It had almost human little hands, with three fingers and a thumb!

Gef let Mrs Irving stroke his fur through a crack in the wall, and put her finger in his mouth.

"His teeth were tiny and sharp," she said. "He drew a little blood from my finger. I told him, 'I don't want any blood poisoning here,' and he replied, 'Go and put ointment on it.' His mouth was about an inch wide."

Sometimes they got a quick view of Gef running along the roof beams, or out-of-doors. But his speed was phenomenal, and terrified of capture, he would scream:

"Damn you, take off your eyes. I can't bear it."

IN 1932, the "Manchester Daily Dispatch" sent a reporter to Cashen's Gap.

"The mysterious 'man-weasel' has spoken to me today," he wrote. "I have heard a voice which I should never have imagined could issue from a human throat.

"The people who claim it was the voice of the strange weasel seem sane, honest and responsible folk and not likely to indulge in a difficult, long-drawn-out and unprofitable practical joke to make themselves the talk of the world."

He left the farm with a tip for the Grand National from Gef! But after a night's sleep, he wrote:

"Does the solution to the mystery lie in the dual personality of the thirteen-year-old girl Voirrey Irving?"

While listening to Gef's "piercing and uncanny voice," the newspaperman had unobtrusively watched Voirrey in a mirror. She had her hand up to her mouth, but her lips did not seem to be moving, and when he drew closer, he saw she was sucking a piece of string.

As their photographs show, the Irvings were a striking-looking family. James Irving had earned a comfortable living before the First World War, but after the war started no-one needed piano salesmen, and in 1915 he put his savings into what was then a prosperous farm.

The farming slump had reduced it to rough grazing for about 30 sheep and a few goats.

But Irving was a cheerful, talkative man, and his wife, Mergery, intelligent and capable. Their only daughter, Voirrey, born in 1918 when the Irvings were already middle-aged, was a quiet, reserved girl, apparently happy to roam the hills with her sheepdog, Mona, and help around the farm.

It must have been a lonely life until Gef focused the attention of the world's Press on the isolated Manx farmhouse.

Gef maintained a love-hate relationship with the family, whose lives he dominated. James Irving

became obsessed with him and began to keep a diary, recording everything he said and did.

He had a healthy appetite and liked biscuits, chocolate, bacon and bananas.

Hearing his shout of "Got a rabbit," the Irvings would find one outside, apparently strangled. During the years, hundreds of rabbits turned up in this way, and Gef also made himself useful, telling Irving where to find lost sheep, or rounding up the goats.

GEF ranged unseen around the island, returning with a fund of gossip, but when Mr Irving repeated Gef's stories to those concerned, he was eyed askance — as they were usually true!

A mechanic at the bus depot at Peel said:

"This animal or whatever it is knows a darn sight too much. He seems to hear what we talk about behind closed doors in the early morning when no-one is about. Mr Irving gave me a perfect description of the inside of my house. He never came to see me and I have never been to Cashen.

"He said Gef told him. It's damn strange."

Gef said he liked to watch the classes through the school windows, and learnt to read this way, often mentioning items he had seen in the newspapers. He also liked to sing hymns, and other, more ribald songs he had picked up.

If the Irvings seldom had more than a quick glimpse of the elusive Gef, sightings by anyone outside the family were rare indeed. But the steady stream of hopeful visitors were often pelted with pebbles or lumps of turf to cries of "Coo-eee."

After a visit by some Irving relatives, Gef reported that on the way home, the visitors suggested that Voirrey was producing Gef's voice by ventriloquism.

"I'll kill their turkeys," he muttered darkly, a threat the Irvings remembered later when they heard their relations had given up poultry farming, as all their turkeys and ducklings had disappeared.

Gef admitted with satisfaction that he was responsible.

Not surprisingly, psychic investigators were eager to visit Cashen's Gap. New York psychiatrist, Dr Nandor Fodor, then Reasearch Officer for the International Institute for Psychical Investigation, spent a week at the farm.

As he said, "A week is a long time in a lonely place," and he felt he had come to know the Irvings really well. He thought they were sincere people, unlikely to carry out a deliberate deception.

There wasn't a squeak out of Gef during the doctor's visit.

Harry Price, the famous psychic investigator, also went to Cashen's Gap in 1935, and like Dr Fodor, found Gef wasn't at home. Apparently he had disappeared after remarking, "Harry Price puts the kibosh on spirits."

During his visit, Price unobtrusively clipped a sample of fur from the sheepdog, Mona, and later had it compared by an expert with a sample Irving said came from Gef. The verdict was that Mona's hair was "absolutely identical with the alleged mongoose hairs."

Voirrey Irving took several snaps of her fleeting encounters with Gef, but they were disappointingly blurred.

Harry Price brought the girl a new camera, and later she took a photograph showing a squirrel-like shape.

It was said to be Gef, but a piece of fur or turf might have looked much the same.

What was the truth about Gef? Neither Fleet Street reporters nor psychic investigators ever managed to expose the amazing talking mongoose as a hoax or fraud. However, some thought that the secret lay with the daughter, Voirrey Irving.

"Is Voirrey in a falsetto voice all there is to Gef?" asked The American Weekly. Gef's arrival had

Continued from page 99

Margy admitted. "He's twenty-nine, and he's tall and dark and — " She paused, and then went on, honestly, "No, not handsome, but nice, Clare."

Ken Johnson *was* nice, Clare had found. He told her, smiling a little, that she probably knew as well as he did why he had been asked tonight, and he had to admit that he had almost had cold feet. But now that he was here, now that he had met her, he was very glad he'd come.

All at once Clare panicked.

"I think I hear Timmy calling," she said, a little breathlessly. "I promised to go up and see him."

Timmy was still awake when she went up to his room.

"I thought you weren't coming," he said reproachfully.

Clare shook her head, and sat down on the bed beside him. "I promised, didn't I?"

He offered her the book he was holding. "Can I have just one little Winnie-the-Pooh story?"

"We mustn't wake Veronica," Clare whispered, opening the book.

She looked across at Veronica, now almost two. She was asleep in her cot with her plump little bottom in the air, and she certainly looked as if nothing would disturb her.

Her voice low, Clare began to read. Before she was halfway through the story she saw that Timmy's eyelids were drooping.

"Don't stop," he said sleepily, when she paused.

Clare went on, only stopping when she saw that he was fast asleep. Gently, she laid him back on his pillow and covered him up. And it was as she turned away from the bed that she saw David standing in the doorway.

He was watching her, with a look in his eyes that stopped her from saying anything at all.

coincided with Voirrey's puberty, and poltergist disturbances have frequently been associated with the presence of an adolescent in the house.

Eventually the farm at Cashen's Gap was sold, and in 1947 the new owner claimed to have shot a strange-looking creature like a mongoose. Was it Gef? Or had he left with the Irvings?

What really happened to the mongoose who so confidently claimed to be the eighth wonder of the world? We shall probably never know. ■

She never knew afterwards how long they stood there with only the dim glow of the nightlight in the small room. But as David looked across at her, unsmiling, she knew why there had been the years of waiting, she knew why no other man had been right for her.

It was so simple, so heartbreakingly simple. She was in love with David, in love with her best friend's husband.

Suddenly, from the party down below, there was a burst of music and laughter. It was enough to break the spell that was binding both of them.

Without a word she walked past him and went downstairs. It was some time before he followed her.

There was a strange unreality about the rest of the evening. When Ken Johnson took her home, she knew that he was disappointed in her lack of response to him.

She slept badly that night. Next morning, although it was cold and grey, she left a note for her father to tell him she had gone for a walk. She went out of the house and along to the beach.

In a way, there was no surprise when David caught up with her.

"I knew you'd be here," he said quietly, and it didn't seem strange to her that he should know that.

They walked along in silence for a while, then he turned to her.

"I'm sorry, Clare," he said. "I — didn't mean you to know — ever."

In spite of the heaviness of her heart, there was a moment of soaring joy. It was the same for him. She hadn't been wrong about last night.

"How long have you known?" she asked him, wonderingly.

He took one of her hands in his and looked down at their fingers entwined.

"A long time," he said at last. His grey eyes met hers and she saw that they were shadowed, from a sleepless night.

"What are we going to do?" she asked him, knowing even as she said it what the answer must be.

"What do you want us to do?" he replied, and the sadness of his voice confirmed what she already knew.

"I'll go away," she said. "It'll be — easier for me to go than for you, and — we can't both stay here."

Neither of them could hurt Margy and the children, and neither of them could contemplate building a future on a broken marriage.

"I've never stopped loving Margy," David told her, and the bewilderment in his voice tore at her heart. "She's my wife, and the mother of my children, and she means so much to me. And yet — I love you, Clare."

The words had been said. They couldn't be taken back.

"I love you, too, David," she whispered.

She didn't know which of them moved first, but suddenly she was in his arms, his lips hard on hers. And when at last he released her, the last of her doubts had gone.

She couldn't stay here in Leymouth, she couldn't risk seeing him. For her own sake, for his, and for Margy's and the children's, she had to go.

They hadn't really said goodbye. They were never alone again, after the moment she parted from him on the beach.

HER father was understanding. He said that he knew she had her own life to live. Margy said much the same, but when she suggested that Clare should come to Leymouth for Christmas, Clare wrote back from London and said that, unfortunately, she wouldn't be able to.

After that first time, it had become easier to make excuses.

Her father was hurt that she didn't come home, but gradually he came to accept it. His visits to her in London kept the contact betwen them.

When she had been away from Leymouth for three years, he decided he would give up the old house and come to live with his sister in a small market town nearer London.

Clare had to go back to Leymouth then to help him to clear the old house, to choose what he could take and what he must leave. She had known that sometime in the three or four days she was to be there, she would see David again.

She wondered, not for the first time, if things would have changed between them, if she would find that now, after all this time, it might be possible for them to see each other without being torn apart.

But the moment she saw him again she knew nothing had changed. There was the same incredible sense of belonging and, although he was careful, she could see it was the same for him.

It hurt, too, seeing Margy again, hearing the reproach in her voice when she talked of the unanswered letters, the invitations turned down.

When she left Leymouth again, Clare had known that in losing the man she loved, she had also lost a dear and close friend. She couldn't possibly continue her friendship with Margy without being continually hurt by the contact with David.

For David and Margy, too, she knew it was better that there should be no reminder for David, no visits, no letters.

As the years went by, she knew their marriage would be good. Margy would never know it had been in danger, and that was the way Clare and David wanted it.

Even so, Clare's certainty grew that for her there could be no-one but David. She didn't avoid contact and meetings with other men, but after an initial attraction, she would find each time that it led to nothing.

The one contact she could not make herself give up was the local newspaper coming once a week with news of Leymouth. She would find David's name fairly often, and sometimes a photograph of him, at school prize-giving, on sports day, at a Rotary dinner.

And there were mentions of the children, too. Because of this, she could picture them growing. The last pictures she had seen of them showed Timmy as a tall 14-year-old with his father's shy smile, holding the cup he had won for running.

And Veronica at 12, in a ballet concert, so changed from the plump baby Clare had held in her arms, that her eyes had blurred with tears as she looked at the picture . . .

ABOVE her, a seagull called mournfully, bringing Clare back to the present. She rose a little stiffly.

No, I can't go to the hospital. If I do, I would destroy everything we have protected for all these years. If — if he dies, he will die knowing that I have spoilt it all, that I wasn't strong enough to keep faith.

If he lives — and he surely must live — he will have to live with what I have done. He will have to spend the rest of his life making it right.

Because nothing can change, now, for us. The things that mattered all those years ago matter just as much now. Margy, the children, his marriage — it was because of them that we parted before, because of them that we knew we had to.

Slowly, she began to walk back to her car. She reached it and paused, still racked with doubt.

How can I go back, she thought, grief-stricken, without even really knowing how he is? "As well as can be expected," they said, but how much or how little does that mean?

The thought that had been in the back of her mind crystallised suddenly.

She could go to Margy. She could go to the house and find out from Margy how David was. She could hear every detail.

Surely Margy wouldn't question her concern for David. She could say she had read of his illness and she came so that she could help with the children while Margy was at the hospital.

She could say that, because of what Margy had done for her when her mother was ill, she couldn't let her face this alone.

With humility, Clare knew that Margy would accept this. But, of course, she would tell David that Clare had come. She would tell him, and whatever the reasons Margy accepted, David would know the real one. *If he still loves me, it can only make it harder for him. And — if he doesn't . . .*

For the first time in all these years she made herself face the thought squarely. David wouldn't have gone back to Margy and his marriage in any half-hearted way. He would have gone back determined to make his marriage work in every way.

He had said, hadn't he, that he had never stopped loving Margy? Being David, he would have been determined to put her out of his mind and his heart, as she herself had gone out of his life. And — he would have succeeded.

The realisation shook her. All these years she had thought of David as a divided man. But David wouldn't compromise. Once she'd gone away, he would put all his strength and all his love into his marriage and his life.

I should have done that, too, Clare thought, with sadness. There had been wasted years, wasted opportunities. Each time she had met someone new, she had closed her mind to him.

Perhaps she might still have found that for her no-one could ever take David's place, but — she knew now that she hadn't given anyone the chance.

I can't go to see Margy, she decided, and she knew that the decision was a step away from the hold of the past. *I'll leave Leymouth without knowing how David is, because I have no right to know. Whatever right I may once have had, I gave up all those years ago, and I have no excuse to cling any longer.*

She could see now, so clearly, that although she had given up the reality of her love for him, she had clung to the memory. Not that she would ever forget her love for him.

But slowly, gropingly, she began to see that she would be able to go forward now, to live her life out of the shadow of her memories.

In a day or two, she promised herself, *I'll phone the hospital again, from London. Perhaps they'll give me more details of how he is.*

It won't matter if the nurse says to Margy that a woman phoned and wouldn't leave her name, because there will be many people phoning, parents of his pupils, old friends. That is all I have the right to do.

Just before she got into her car, Clare looked back down at the deserted beach. The tide was almost in now and her footprints were almost obliterated, the sea breaking over them in white foam.

Tonight, she thought, *when the tide goes out again, the sand where I walked will be smooth and untouched, ready for new footprints, ready for a new beginning.*

——————— ∗ **THE END** ∗ ———————

LITTLE THINGS MEAN A LOT

. . . And to one old lady they turned a birthday full of disappointment into a day she would always treasure.

A S she went downstairs to pick up the paper and the morning's post, Mrs Jordan wrapped her flowered dressing-gown more tightly round her. It was chilly in the little hall after the warmth and cosiness of her bedroom, or perhaps, she wondered, you felt the cold more when you were getting on a bit.

She bent to retrieve her paper — a luxury these days, but it was one of her small treats she gave

**Complete Story
by EILEEN ELIAS**

herself, living on a pension. Then, after the slightest pause, she bent to pick up the card lying on the mat.

She knew it was no use supposing it was a birthday card — even though it *was* her birthday. She'd reconciled herself to that by now.

Gazing at the ceiling from her bed that morning, she'd realised, with something of a shock, that this year there wouldn't even be a card from Hilda. Always, even after her husband's death, there had been Hilda — dear, faithful friend Hilda, who never forgot.

But now Hilda had gone the way of all the others.

No, she told herself firmly and sensibly, there wouldn't be any birthday mail today.

Still, there was something — a card from the library. That book she'd ordered about Japan had just come in. Good — that would make something to read this afternoon, when she put her feet up. A real birthday treat.

A few minutes later, as she made tea in the tiny kitchen, Mrs Jordan smiled to herself as she remembered Japan. Those had been the days, when, with dear Denis at her side, she'd spent a whole delightful, unforgettable year in Japan.

Dear Denis.

Denis Jordan had been her own Dear Denis for the rest of his life. For so long he'd been there to give her his special birthday kiss and the little surprise he'd saved up for. Right to the end Denis had been a boy at heart, always one for a surprise.

Mrs Jordan filled her teapot and put it on the breakfast tray laid out the night before, ready to carry up to the warm bedroom. Breakfast in bed — another little luxury now she was alone.

When she went back up to her room, she glanced at the silver-framed photograph she always kept by her bed. Dear Denis. How she missed him now on special days. Christmas and birthdays were hard to get through without him.

Oh, she knew she was lucky, really. She had a little house, just enough energy to get about, friends, the church on Sundays — but there were still times when she longed for the sound of his voice, the touch of his hand.

Times, too, when she'd all but heard him speaking, as she lay in the big bed in the lonely hours, just before morning. And once, she'd thought she'd felt the brush of his lips on her cheek. But it had only been a moth flying in from the open window to flutter round the lamplight.

She'd remembered what Denis had once told her — that a moth fluttering at the window was one of the departed, trying to get in. Just a fancy, of course, nothing more. But it had, so very nearly, been the touch of Denis's kiss against a cheek that was old now, and furrowed.

Propped up on pillows, Mrs Jordan poured herself a second cup of tea and turned over the library card in her hand. Nice of them to let me know like that, wasn't it? Then, of course, she knew people *were* nice in Grayfield — even though she'd only lived there a year or two.

She often had a word with the lady at the corner shop, and the man at the post office where she drew her pension was kind.

Then there were the children who were always out playing by the pond in the Quadrant. And someone always chatted to her after church.

Once a lad from the Church Youth Club had even called to ask whether she wanted her front hedge cutting. She'd given him tea and one of her currant scones, even though he had looked so strange, with his stubbly hair and patched jeans. Perhaps if she'd had children of her own his appearance wouldn't have been so strange.

Denis would have laughed, she told herself now, pushing aside her breakfast tray and revelling in the last few moments in bed.

"Times change," he'd have told her.

Well, that was true enough. This was her birthday morning, and how different it was from the ones she used to know! But it didn't do any good to think about those.

If she got up now, she decided, while the morning was fine, she could walk round to the library and get that book about Japan. Then there'd be something to look forward to after dinner, when she would put her feet up and have a nice long read. She could go back for an hour or two to Japan — and almost fancy she and Denis were back there together again.

What a time they'd had — the temples, the little tinkling bells and those tiny Japanese ladies who looked like smiling dolls.

That wonderful year when Denis had been on business in Tokyo, and she'd been young enough and active enough to go anywhere with him.

Yes, Mrs Jordan thought, rousing herself from bed and fumbling for her slippers beneath it, she mustn't grumble. She'd had a happy life. She was one of the lucky ones — even now.

IT was nice to walk down to the library, Mrs Jordan told herself, as she stepped out as briskly as she could. The first bit, before the houses got so numerous, was really quite like the countryside where Denis and she had lived together.

Even now, Grayfield had a field or two left, and a gate where horses leaned their heads. They always watched for her coming, just like friends.

As she neared them, Mrs Jordan fished in her handbag for the two lumps of sugar she always kept there. An extravagance, perhaps, but then, the horses were like people to her, and she had grown to love them.

Well, she thought, you'd give a friend two lumps of sugar in her tea, wouldn't you, even on a pension?

She felt the soft nuzzle of the velvety lips against the palm of her hand, and smiled to herself as she went on her way.

Now the houses were closer. She passed by the new Parade, and the post office and the little shops, and came to the Quadrant, where the library stood.

There were children playing by the pond. Good, she thought, that would be somebody else to talk to. And before that she'd have a word with nice Mrs Brady who had sent her the card about the book.

Really, it was quite as good as a birthday card, she told herself, as she climbed the three low steps to the swing doors of the library. Well, nearly . . .

Behind the "Reserved Books" counter, little Mrs Brady was looking a shade worried this morning, Mrs Jordan thought. In fact, she quite often looked worried and Mrs Jordan supposed it was that Ken of hers. So many marriages seemed troubled these days.

There were circles smudged under Mrs Brady's eyes and, more than once lately, she'd seen the signs of Mrs Brady's sleepless nights. There'd been a day last week when the woman had been near to tears.

"I can't take much more, Mrs Jordan," she'd whispered. "For two pins I'd . . ."

But whatever she'd intended to do, she hadn't.

Mrs Jordan smiled. Well, I did at least provide a listening ear at the right moment then, she thought.

Mrs Jordan smiled again.

"Lovely morning," she said, taking no notice of Mrs Brady's heavy eyelids. She'd talk if she wanted to.

But at the sound of the old lady's voice, tears swam in Mrs Brady's eyes. She fumbled on the shelf behind her for the book on Japan, and kept her face down so Mrs Jordan wouldn't see.

"Oh dear, Ken again, is it?" Mrs Jordan laid a timid hand on her arm. "I know. They *can* be trying, sometimes. Even dear Denis . . ." Mrs Jordan pulled herself up quickly. Oh, forgive me, please, she thought quickly. Dear Denis was *never* trying. But then, she realised, she was one of the lucky ones.

"I've made up my mind," Mrs Brady was whispering, looking round to see that nobody else was near. "This time — this is really it . . ."

"I remember saying that," Mrs Jordan said gently. "I really meant it, too, that day. Such a row we had, but by next morning it had all simmered down again, and when I woke up the sun was shining, like it is today. Things never seem quite so bad in the morning. Is that my book on Japan, dear?"

Mrs Brady managed a wavery smile.

That's right, Mrs Jordan thought. She won't walk out — today at any rate. She flicked open the pages of the book.

"This looks lovely," she said. "Thank you so much for getting it for me. Keep smiling, Mrs Brady. There's always the morning after, you know."

And as she pushed open the doors on her way out of the library, Mrs Jordan thought that she wouldn't like to see Mrs Brady becoming one of the lonely ones. She simply wasn't the type.

Some children run the risk of growing up in social isolation.

The best way to put a stop to this is to give a party.

thelwell's
BRAT RACE
HOW TO GIVE A PARTY

Never invite more youngsters than you can comfortably cope with.

Children get very pre-occupied with the food —

— So warn them to leave room for the trifle.

Try to restrict the party to the garden if possible.

Make quite sure the children know when the party's over.

H

113

Children have very definite opinions on what it is they like to play with.

Observe the kind of games that give them the most pleasure.

And they adore being given real tools —

— Which they quickly learn how to use.

MRS JORDAN crossed the Quadrant towards the pond for a nice sit-down. It was something to do, to watch the youngsters playing.

She and Denis hadn't been blessed with children, but then, perhaps, that very fact had drawn them closer together.

Things usually worked out somehow, didn't they? Mrs Jordan sat back on a bench in the sunshine and watched a small boy standing alone. He was new here, she realised, she'd never seen him before.

He wasn't playing with the others. He was just standing alone, scuffing the gravel with the toe of his sandal. It was a "don't care" sort of gesture that meant he does care a lot, really, Mrs Jordan thought.

Two boys were sailing a boat on the pond, and another was running up and down the bank, but this one didn't join in.

She felt in her handbag for the cough sweets she usually carried. Then she smiled.

"Like one of these?" she asked.

The boy edged closer warily. He eyed her with caution, then took the sweet from her with a grubby hand.

"Thanks," he muttered.

"Not playing with the others?" Mrs Jordan's tone was casual.

He didn't answer, but kicked a stone on the path.

thelwell's BRAT RACE

TOYS AND PRESENTS

It is a mistake to give presents which you yourself would like to own.

Remember to test all toys yourself before purchase to make quite sure they are in perfect working order.

"Don't you like sailing boats, then?" she asked.

He turned and looked at her.

"Mmm." He nodded.

"Not playing with the others?"

He shook his head.

"They don't want me," he said.

Mrs Jordan looked at him.

"You're new to Grayfield, aren't you? Only just come?" she asked.

"Mmmm," he whispered, and that, thought Mrs Jordan, explained a lot.

She gazed out over the pond, and the boy's stare followed her.

"Fine boat they've got there," Mrs Jordan said, narrowing her eyes.

"Not bad." He paused a moment. "My dad's a sailor."

"Is he now? That's interesting." Mrs Jordan's face lit up. "When my husband was alive, we once went on a boat all the way to Japan. It was wonderful. I'll never forget it."

'My dad's been to Japan. My dad's been everywhere," the boy said.

He was sitting on the bench beside her now, swinging his legs.

"When my dad comes home in two months, Mum says he'll build

115

me a boat of my own. A proper boat — better than that."

He pointed to the boat on the pond with wistful eyes.

"Well, now," Mrs Jordan said. "Isn't that grand? Let's go over and see what they're doing at the pond, shall we?"

She smiled as a small hand slipped into hers.

The two of them stood quite a while in silence, admiring the boat as it sped with the light wind across the pond. Then Mrs Jordan spoke to the boy nearest to her.

"Do you know," she said conversationally, "this lad here — what did you say your name was?"

"Tom."

"Tom here — his dad's a sailor."

The boy looked up, first at her, then at Tom. It was a look of appraisal.

"And when he comes home next time," Mrs Jordan went on, "he's going to build Tom a boat to sail on this pond. That'll be fun for all of you, won't it?"

Several pairs of eyes turned to them, and she noticed a gleam in them.

"What sort of boat's your dad on?" a voice asked.

"Submarine," Tom said proudly. "He's in submarines."

"Great!" There was a ripple of admiration. "Tell us about the submarines."

Mrs Jordan left Tom telling them, and at the corner of the Quadrant she turned to see Tom's arms outstretched as he explained some point, and the others were grouped round him.

She smiled. He was "in" at last. There was no doubt about that.

Denis would have been glad, she thought, walking home. Denis always had a soft spot for children.

WHEN she got home, the little house was quiet. She sat down in the kitchen and took off her shoes.

Walking was tiring these days, even just to the Quadrant and back. But the sun had been nice, and she'd enjoyed those little chats.

Well, she decided, now for lunch. In the old days it would have been Denis who cooked her birthday lunch. Who said a man couldn't be good at cooking? Denis's birthday lunches were wonderful.

Today — well, there were some eggs in the larder, and what could be better than poached eggs on toast — and a nice cup of tea?

After dinner she had a little nap, then the book on Japan passed another hour or two. It was good to get carried away like this.

What a wonderful thing the library was, Mrs Jordan thought. She didn't know how she'd have managed the last year or two without Mrs Brady and her choice of books.

She looked at the clock. Nearly four — teatime already? And a thought struck her.

Denis always remembered to order her a birthday cake from the baker's on the corner. Pride of place it had always taken, on the table with the white cloth and the best china. Denis would have smiled as he watched her cut the first slice.

Ah, well, that was a long time ago, and Denis was wrong. You *did* grow old . . .

However, she thought, she wasn't too old to bake a cake — that was a knack you never lost.

Then another thought came to her — a different one this time. Why not bake a birthday cake for somebody else?

She'd noticed the poster on the Vicarage gate as she passed on her way from the library. The Youth Club, wasn't it, needing things for some sort of party evening — a disco, whatever that was?

Mrs Jordan smiled. She knew what she would do . . .

The sponge came out of the oven sweet-smelling and softly brown. Mrs Jordan, her back aching a little from standing so long, set it to cool in the larder while she made herself a cup of tea.

In the evening she'd ice it and take it across to the Vicar. It was only a step to the Vicarage so it wouldn't take a minute.

WHEN she arrived at the Vicarage that evening, the Vicar himself opened the door.

"Why, it's Mrs Jordan! How nice to see you!" he said, smiling, and his voice so like Denis's at that moment that Mrs Jordan's head swam a little.

She stepped into the cool, shadowy hall, where a bowl of garden flowers stood on a polished chest. Silently, she held out the cake, in its wrapping of greaseproof paper.

"Not for me, surely?" the vicar was saying, clearly surprised.

Mrs Jordan laughed.

"Well, not exactly," she said. "It's just that I saw this morning the Youth Club was wanting gifts for the — the —"

"Ah, yes, the disco," they Vicar said, leading the way into his pleasant sitting-room.

"That's very kind of you," he went on. "Any contributions are extremely welcome, you know."

He studied her thoughtfully as she settled in the armchair. "I'm surprised, really, though, Mrs Jordan. The Youth Club — it's not . . . well, your sort of scene, is it? So many people here in Grayfield seem to rather resent the Youth Club. Wouldn't dream of supporting it unless they had to."

She noticed the tired look in his eyes, and the little frown on his forehead.

"Of course, I don't know anything about . . . discos, Vicar," she said, "but a very nice boy from your club once came to cut the hedge for me. Without my asking, too. Oh, no, I don't think anyone could resent the Youth Club. Fine lot of young people, I'd say."

The Vicar's frown lifted and his eyes looked less tired.

"Funny you should say that, Mrs Jordan," he said. "I was saying to my wife only this morning that sometimes I wonder if it's any good going on with the Youth Club. Nobody seemed to take any interest in it. In fact, I was seriously considering closing it down. But now you've put heart into me."

His eyes turned to Mrs Jordan's cake, standing in its white wrappings on the mahogany table.

"It's only a little thing," she said, humbly.

"Sometimes it's the little things that turn the tide," the Vicar said. Then he paused for a moment. "Zechariah, four, ten, isn't it? *Who hath despised the day of small things?*"

"The day of small things," Mrs Jordan echoed, then she realised that was just exactly what her day had been like.

Not like those other birthdays of old, full of events and happenings, but a day of small things — and each had brought her joy. She had a lot to be thankful for.

In the hall, as she said goodbye, Mrs Jordan studied the Vicar's face. He looked much less tired now, she thought. Poor man, it must be hard work running the parish — and the Youth Club as well. Fancy even thinking of closing it down! That would never do.

She was glad he'd liked the cake. It was the next best thing to having a birthday cake of her own.

IT was twilight when she crossed the road to her own front door. She let herself in, hearing the hollowness of her footsteps in the empty hall.

She turned on the light and made herself a cup of tea, remembering that she had the book on Japan to read before she went to bed. It would be a nice way to finish the day.

She took her supper tray into the sitting-room, sat down in her chair, and prepared to settle for a read over her sandwich and tea.

Then she realised she didn't have her spectacles, and she needed them these days. She needed the reading lamp, too.

Reaching across, she turned on the switch.

The lamplight sprang into golden warmth as Mrs Jordan reviewed her day. There hadn't been any birthday cards, but she'd had that card from the library, and exchanged a chat with Mrs Brady.

She hadn't travelled very far — not like long ago — but she'd sat by the pond and enjoyed those children with their boats — yes, and little Tom.

She hadn't exactly had a celebration tea, but she *had* had a birthday cake — a proper one, with icing on top, even if it had been given to someone else.

Small things, but happy ones. What was it the Vicar had said? *Who hath despised the day of small things?*

Suddenly there was a tiny sound at the window beside her, a sound of fluttering against the glass, and she knew what it was.

Of course, it was only a fancy, she told herself, remembering what dear Denis used to say. All the same, she opened the window just a chink — to let the moth fly in.

——————— * **THE END** * ———————

"AND I QUOTE . . ."

Eric Bartholomew (1926-84) took the
name Morecambe from his home town.
He began his career in a youth show, where he met Ernie Wise.
They formed a long-lived comic partnership, particularly notable on
TV. Ernest Wiseman (1925-), born in Yorkshire, performed in
working men's clubs before joining Eric.

*That Japanese chap gets
up really high when he's
vaulting. It's what is
known as a nip in the air.*

*Lew Grade wasn't a Lord
then — just "Your
Majesty."*

*My watch has stopped.
But it's still right twice a
day.*

*Ladies and gentlemen,
welcome to the show.
We want you to relax
and enjoy
yourselves . . . and if
you don't laugh there's a
spike that comes up out
of the seat.*

*She was wearing a going-
away dress. It looked like
part of it had already left.*

*We wouldn't go on to
the stage to perform to
half-empty houses. Half-
full ones, yes, perhaps.*

*The first Royal Command performance we performed in,
we chased a girl wearing a grass skirt across the stage with
a lawn-mower.*

Complete Story by
ELIZABETH ASHCROFT

JENNIFER BARRETT peered anxiously through the windscreen at the drifting, treacherous fog.

Rod, driving, muttered something under his breath, and she turned on him impulsively.

"You would come today! We could easily have left tomorrow. We could have taken our time instead of rushing here like maniacs — just so you could fit in an extra day's business!"

He sighed with exasperation, driving close to the verge, squinting painfully as a lorry veered from nowhere and just missed them.

"We've been through all this before, Jennifer. It was just an unexpected chance to look round the place, before I say yes or no to the job. Now, can we leave it? It's difficult enough trying to drive in this weather, without you going on at me all the time!"

She hunched in the corner of her seat, stifling a pang of sympathy at Rod's drawn face. He hated driving in fog, and she wondered vaguely whether she should take over. But one glance at his tense, angry face warned her to keep quiet.

In the uncomfortable silence that followed, she wished he'd never even told her about this new job.

It was just three days ago, she realised. They had been sitting after supper, the children in bed. She'd thought Rod had seemed quiet all evening.

She'd begun telling him about Pat next door's new extension to the house.

"It's made it so much bigger. They're going to use it as a small sitting-room. Pat said we can go over and see it tomorrow.

"Really, Rod, it's a great idea. We could build out the back, too. We could afford it — and it would give us so much more room."

Rod had hesitated. "I don't think so, Jennifer," he'd said quietly.

"Why not?" she'd asked.

"Well, love. It's just that we might have to move."

"*Move*? But we can't!" she'd exclaimed.

For the past nine years they'd lived in their square, solid house, and she'd put all her energy and love into it. All her friends were here. The twins went to school just down the road. They couldn't move — they couldn't!

"We may have to," Rod had said drily. "There's a job as under-manager in the Welsh factory. It's a terrific opportunity. The whole place needs re-organising."

"And you want to go?" she'd asked incredulously. "You want to go and live in — in Wales, of all places?"

She'd been to Wales once before, for a camping holiday with Rod

FOLLOW OUR DREAM

**That's how their marriage had began. Now
they both realised that somewhere
along the way reality had set in . . .**

when they were first married. Wales to her was a memory of green
hills and rain, and leaking tents and soaking wellington boots.

In all the 15 years of their marriage they had worked and fought
together to get where they were. They were settled now — they had
the security of the house, her mother lived not far away, and now he
wanted to throw it all away!

"Rod, I don't want to live in Wales!" she'd cried, and to her utter
horror tears had sprung into her eyes.

"It means more money," he'd said distantly. "We could have that
caravan we wanted, and a bigger house."

"I thought you liked living here, Rod. You said only the other day

121

how nice it was to have so many friends in such a nice neighbourhood!"

He'd sighed, shrugging. "That was before this job came up.
Circumstances change, Jennifer. I was settled, in a rut. Now, this job
seems — well, exciting.

"Consider it, Jennifer. I have to go up there on Thursday, so come
with me? See what you think of the place."

"If I have to come to see it," she'd said stiffly, "why can't we go
for a weekend instead of rushing there and taking me along as an
afterthought? There won't be time for me to see anything, if you've
got to see lots of people all day."

"You can look around the estate agents," he'd informed her, his
blue eyes cold. "Buy the local papers, see what property is like.

"Jennifer," his voice had softened, "remember when we were first
married? I had to move after we'd only been married two months,
and we had that dreadful basement flat. You thought that was an
adventure."

"It was!" she'd cried. "But I was only twenty then and everything
was an adventure. We didn't have children, or — the house, or — or
other ties."

"You're right!" he'd answered swiftly. "The house is a tie. So is
the garden! But you're so fond of them you don't want to leave
them. You won't take a chance any more, Jennifer. You like your
comfort too much."

IT wasn't true, she thought now, huddling inside the car. She didn't
like her comforts too much. It was just that she was older and
more settled.

A twinge of fear touched her as she glanced at Rod's set face. Ever
since this job had come up, he'd become a stranger.

"We won't be at the hotel in time," he said quietly. "And they'll
let someone else have the room, more than likely. We'll have to find
somewhere else."

"Somewhere else?" Her voice rose. "In this wilderness?"

She peered out at the damp swirling fog, getting thicker by the
minute.

"Don't argue, Jennifer. Let me concentrate. It's getting worse, and
we're into the hills again."

She sat tense while he cautiously negotiated the bends in the roads.
Her legs were stiff and aching, her back was sore.

She thought with a touch of shame that Rod must be feeling far
worse. If only they could find a hotel, somewhere to stop and rest.

Then quite suddenly they came upon a little village.

Rod sounded relieved. "Maybe there's a hotel here. I'll have to
stop anyway. I can't go on any longer."

THEY crawled along the deserted village high street, and Jennifer's
heart sank. There was nothing that remotely resembled a hotel.

Then Rod stopped next to a little sign, swinging over a hedge.

It looked old and grimy and the letters were crooked.

Bed And Breakfast.

Vacancies.

I bet there are vacancies, Jennifer thought grimly, peering at the overgrown garden and the forbidding house. She turned to Rod, and to her astonishment he was unfastening his seat belt.

"Rod, we can't!" she began, but he interrupted firmly.

"Jennifer, maybe you'd rather spend the night in the car, but I wouldn't. It may not be a three-star hotel, but there will be a bed, and with luck, a meal. I'm going to see if they'll have us."

He came back down the path, and she saw how tired he was after the long drive. Again guilt touched her.

He put his head in the door. "Bit of luck. They've got a room. Grab your suitcase."

And he was gone, leaving her to get her own suitcase and lock the car.

Biting her lip and fighting back tears, she followed him into the narrow hall. It was so dark she could hardly see the woman waiting for them. There was a smell of bacon in the air, and a definite feeling of dampness.

"Welcome," the woman said, in a lilting voice. "Although it's not much of a welcome you'll be getting today in this weather, is it?"

As she spoke, she led the way up the creaking, narrow stairs to a small bedroom. She ushered them in.

"Will you be wanting a meal?" she asked.

Rod spoke quickly, his voice warm for the first time all day.

"Yes, please! If it's no trouble."

"Fine," she said. "I expect you'd like a wash, so I'll bring you up some hot water."

Then she was gone.

"Bring us some hot water!" Jennifer exclaimed. "You mean to say there isn't even any hot water!"

His voice was distant again. "You heard the lady. Not everyone has all mod. cons."

There was a knock on the door.

"Water," the low, singsong voice said.

Rod took it in. There was a glimmer of laughter in his face as he turned to Jennifer.

"Just like Great-Grandma's day," he said, taking the enormous flowered jug over to the matching washbowl. "I would never have believed it if I hadn't seen it!"

He splashed his face with hot water, pushing back his damp hair.

Suddenly, he looked younger, more vulnerable. Not like the harried businessman of late.

He added, bitterly, "Maybe you don't need so much up here. You live closer to nature, watch the seasons come and go. No Pat and her extensions on one side, and Jane and her parties on the other."

Jennifer flushed. She realised that for a long time now, she and Rod had gone their own ways, she with her friends, Rod with his.

THE meal was simple, wholesome and nourishing, and Rod loved it.

"Real, old-fashioned, home-cooking," he enthused.

Jennifer thought of her deep-freeze stacked with expensive convenience food, so that she could be free to shop with Pat and visit Jane.

"Now what do we do?" she asked, as Mrs Evans, their hostess, put a homely brown teapot before her and left them alone.

Rod looked surprised. "Sit. And talk, I suppose."

"With Mrs Evans?" she inquired.

He nodded pleasantly. "Nice woman. Has a hard time, I imagine.

"Jennifer," he appealed to her suddenly, "can't you try to make the best of it? I know it's not your idea of a night out, but it could be worse, you know."

"Not much," she retorted, rising. "I'm tired. I'm going to bed."

Once upstairs, she got into bed quickly. It was cold here, for early September. She left the curtains open so she could see the sky and suddenly, as she squirmed and fidgeted on the lumpy mattress, she remembered her first holiday in Wales when she and Rod had finally been flooded out of their tent.

They had spent the night in their old banger of a car. They had curled up on the back seat, steam rising from their damp clothes where the tent had collapsed on top of them.

Rod had lost his temper as she'd scurried round trying to salvage pots and food and bits of clothes.

"I don't want you catching pneumonia!" he'd said forcefully, and he'd bundled her into the car.

He wouldn't be so concerned now, she thought wistfully, remembering how relieved she had been to give up, to collapse on his shoulder, shivering, in the cramped confines of the car. They hadn't slept at all that night, just lain there close to each other, watching the dawn come, a blaze of pink and gold over the hills.

"Oh," she'd said, gasping at the sheer glory of it. "It was worth it, just for that! It was," she'd added, turning to him, "an adventure!"

"It's all an adventure," he'd answered, kissing the tip of her nose. "The whole of life is an adventure, my lovely Jen, and it always will be so long as we're together."

And that sense of adventure had gone, she thought suddenly, sitting bolt upright in the narrow bumpy bed.

THERE was the sound of feet on the stairs, and unaccountably her heart began to thud. The door opened slowly, and Rod came in. Not eagerly as he had done in the first years of their marriage, but with a measured, quiet tread.

Her Rod, who was going to hitch-hike to Katmandu, who once in a mad moment had painted the whole kitchen scarlet, who had taken her camping to Spain, because it was the only way they could afford it. Rod, whose dream was to go to India.

Or was it? She wondered suddenly. Did Rod still have dreams? She didn't really know her husband any more. The thought dismayed her.

"Rod?" She spoke into the darkness, seeing his figure halt in surprise. "Do you still want to go to India?"

He looked oddly vulnerable as he came towards her. In the fitful moonlight she saw a strangely wistful expression on his face.

"I shall always want to go. Even when I'm an old, old man, I shall dream of India."

He shook his head. "It's too late now. I shall never get there."

"Yes, you will!" She spoke forcefully and he stepped back, surprised.

"You'll go anywhere you want to, Rod! You're like that! I'd even —" she hesitated. "I'd come with you."

"You would?" He sounded astonished. "You'd come to India? And you don't want to come to Wales?"

She wondered if he would remember.

"I was remembering," she said slowly, "that night we spent in the car when we were flooded out of the tent. You said to be anywhere with me would be an adventure. It isn't any more, is it? Because of me.

"I've been submerged in being a housewife. I've forgotten there's more to life than — than hot water, and — and bigger houses, and a deep-freeze."

Suddenly his hand touched hers. "It could still be an adventure, Jen," he whispered.

It was the first time he'd called her that for months, she realised.

"It's partly my fault," he continued. "I should have told you how I was feeling. I shouldn't have sprung this move on you so suddenly. And, Jen, we won't have to do without your mod. cons!

"It's just the change I need, love. A new challenge, in a new job. A feeling of satisfaction. I thought — you might feel the same, too."

To her astonishment, she did.

"I do feel the same," she said unexpectedly. "All of a sudden, I do. I want to come, Rod. We'll find an old house, and we'll be self-supporting. I'll grow my own vegetables — maybe we could even have a — a goat."

"A goat!" He gave a great shout of laughter. "You'll be making your own butter next."

"Why not?" she asked stoutly. "Rod, I'm sorry. It's been a dreadful day, and I haven't helped at all. In fact, I've been utterly selfish and I'm so ashamed."

Suddenly his arms were round her, holding her comfortingly close.

"No need, Jen. I've been selfish, too, trying to will you here by sheer brute force."

He kissed her gently. "It will be an adventure, my love, you'll see!"

——————— * **THE END** * ———————

The fox and the St Bernard. That's how she thought of the two men in her life. No wonder they were going —

ANIMAL CRACKERS!

MORNA DAVIS had just moved the model of Hoppy the Rabbit over beside the plastic tree stump when a movement outside the store window caught her eye.

A smartly-dressed young man with longish, dark hair stood on the pavement scowling in at her.

Usually, when young men showed an interest in her window-dressing activities, she cheerfully discouraged them by making faces before finally blocking their view in some way or other. But instinct told her that this young man was not just an ordinary passer-by.

She scowled back at him.

The cheek! He was actually signalling to her to move Hoppy the Rabbit to the other side of the window. He was flapping his hands about like the flippers on an agitated sea-lion.

She smiled to herself at the comparison she'd made. Ever since her schooldays she'd had a capacity for likening people to animals.

She looked again at the young man. His scowl had gone, but there was no mistaking his deep disgust.

A few minutes later, when she had finished the window and was walking towards the lift, she saw her tormentor crossing the floor to cut her off.

"Just what were you playing at in that window?" he demanded.

"What's it to do with you?" Morna replied, equally curtly. "Look, I've spent half the afternoon trying to improve a window lay-out designed by some bright boy with as much imagination as the gates on this lift!

"Now if that's answered your question," Morna went on, "I'm off to the canteen for a welcome cup of tea. Excuse me."

She smiled icily and stepped into the lift.

But before she could do anything about it the stranger had got into the lift beside her.

*Complete
Story
by
IAN
S. CLARK*

"Perhaps *I* don't have any more imagination than the gates on this lift," he said mildly, "but I expect *my* window lay-outs to be carried out as I designed them!"

MORNA groaned. His distinct arty appearance should have warned her. Pensive, sensitive brown eyes, about 25 years old. Morna groaned again. He could only be the new whizz-kid of Art and Publicity. She had heard of him but hadn't been through to head office to meet him yet.

"N . . . Nicholas Haddock?" she said nervously.

"Haddow," he corrected her. "I spent a lot of time working on that design to get it exactly right, and I don't like to see it ruined by the whim of some window-dresser."

"It wasn't a whim," Morna argued. "It was instinct . . . experience. It looked much better the way I did it."

He snorted angrily and began to say something — only to be interrupted by the lift stopping at the third floor.

"Look, Mr Haddow," she said calmly. "Don't you see that doesn't necessarily mean you've a better eye for display than anyone else!

"Experience counts for a lot, you know," she added as they made their way to the canteen.

"But Hoppy should flank the display and look as if he's rushing into the shop," he said stubbornly.

Morna shrugged impatiently. "Your predecessor allowed us a lot of scope, and this isn't the first time I've improved a display."

"That was his affair!"

"All right then, I'll change the display," she said emphatically. "But it will upset my schedule completely for the rest of the afternoon. I'll have to work late and I'll be late for my date."

He stopped to hold the canteen door open for her. "Er . . . well perhaps, just this once . . ." he said, following her inside.

"Oh, no — I insist!"

Morna was beginning to enjoy her martyred rôle. He was on the defensive now and looking guilty.

"Perhaps I could get you coffee?" he asked.

"No, thanks," Morna answered coolly. "My friend's over there. If you'll excuse me, I'll join him. I don't suppose he'll be too pleased when I tell him I'll have to work late."

Morna's statement had quite a shattering effect on him. His forehead furrowed and his chin drooped. Morna thought suddenly he looked like a troubled St Bernard dog. In fact, the longer she looked at him the more she could see him with a brandy cask around his neck.

Morna turned away triumphantly and made for Ted Sturrock's table. Ted was the only person she knew in the canteen.

She saw his eyes widen with pleasure when she realised she was about to sit beside him. He stood up gallantly and held a chair for her.

"This is a pleasure!" he said and smiled. "I was beginning to think I was wasting my time on you."

She sat down and returned his smile warmly, hoping that Mr Nicholas Haddow was watching.

"Not entirely," she said.

"Then maybe I could persuade you to come out for dinner or to a show some evening?" Ted suggested hopefully. "And what could be better than this evening?"

Morna knew Ted's type — suave, in his early 30s, a junior executive — and an incorrigible chaser of attractive girls.

She pictured him as a handsome, sophisticated fox — the type you might see in a cartoon film luring the unsuspecting chicken from its roost.

"I'm sorry, I'm pretty well booked up over the next two weeks," she lied.

"Shame. Can't persuade you to change your mind?"

" 'Fraid not." She laughed in a tone she hoped would sound affectionate. "Maybe another time."

She talked teasingly, laughing into his eyes — completely puzzling him until at length out of the corner of her eye she saw Nicholas Haddow get up and leave. He did so without casting a glance in her direction.

As for Ted, she knew that he thought he was making a terrific impression on her and that a date was imminent. She didn't bother to disillusion him, and laughed inwardly when she imagined herself as the unsuspecting chicken that Ted was trying to lure away.

"I really must be going," she said. "I've got to do that window again. Our artistic friend from head office wasn't too impressed by the alterations I made to his design."

Ted grinned. "Typical head office type. I sympathise."

THAT evening, as she climbed to her bedsitter, Morna felt slightly depressed. The fact was, she hadn't been on a date for quite a while.

At first, when she came to the city, over a year ago, everything had been so new and exciting.

She was more discriminating now about her dates and spent a lot of her evenings reading, or watching television.

Tonight, however, her home-made meal contrasted poorly with the meal she might have had if she'd accepted Ted's invitation. Maybe he was a bit of a wolf, but she thought a date with him could have been good fun.

Briefly she let herself think of her triumph over Nicholas Haddow — but even that had lost its savour.

The next few days she spent dressing windows in one of the firm's other branches, but it wasn't until the next week that she returned to the store where Ted worked. It was to arrange a "Summer Siesta" scene — which she did with meticulous care, right down to the last colourful umbrella.

"That's fine. Yes . . . really good."

She turned from arranging the last touches of the scene to find

Nicholas Haddow watching.

"It's your design," she said coldly. "Did you come to spy on me?"

"No, I didn't," he answered. "I had something else in mind."

"Oh?" Morna was puzzled.

"I thought you might like to enter an idea for our next Children's Sale," he explained. "We're working on it at head office, but I know from the files that you've made some good suggestions in the past. I'd like to encourage that sort of thing, so we're turning it into a sort of competition.

"There will be a bonus for each suggestion submitted and something quite substantial for the winner."

"That sounds great," Morna said, despite herself. She loved doing that sort of thing. "Well, I'm off for coffee now and I'll see if I get any inspiration."

"I . . . I'm just going for a coffee myself," he put in hurriedly. "I'll come up with you."

"OK," Morna said.

Over coffee he apologised for the argument they'd had on their last meeting.

"I hope your boyfriend wasn't too put out," he said, embarrassed. "I hope the window didn't keep you too long."

"Er . . . no. It didn't take as long as I thought." She blushed.

He quickly changed the subject, and from time to time Morna found herself studying him.

There was a gentle understanding in his deep brown eyes, she thought with surprise. And a few minutes later, she actually found herself thinking it might be nice to be asked out by Nicholas Haddow.

She had just finished her coffee when Ted walked into the canteen. His eyes brightened when he spotted her.

"Ah, our artistic friend from head office — who didn't like your improvements." Ted beamed at her roguishly.

"Er . . . this is Ted Sturrock," she said hastily. "Ted . . . Nicholas Haddow."

"How do you do?" Nicholas smiled. "Nice to meet you but I'm afraid I must be getting back."

He glanced at Morna. "You'll remember the competition, won't you, Miss Davis? I'll be looking for something special."

"Yes . . . of course. I'll do my best."

HE must have second sight," Ted said as Nicholas closed the canteen door behind him. "This time I won't be put off. I'll just keep on asking you until you agree to a date."

Sitting there, Morna remembered how lonely she had felt after her last visit to the store and how she had wished she had accepted Ted's date then.

"Well," Ted asked, "shall I pick you up at your place around seven on Saturday night?"

"Yes, that'll be fine," Morna agreed.

She spent every evening that week trying to think up an idea for the window design competition, but nothing really original came to mind.

Ted called for her just a little after seven on Saturday, and took her to a little club which had dancing and a cabaret act. But all his cheerful banter was lost on her as they sat together at a corner table.

She tried desperately to concentrate on what he was saying, but every so often thoughts for the window display would sidle into her head. Several times Ted had to repeat himself.

"You know, this is very daunting," he said. "My reputation for making girls fall at my feet could suffer a very serious setback. You're shattering my confidence."

"I'm sorry, Ted," she apologised. "A work problem. I can't get it out of my head. I'm trying to think up a really good design for a window display."

"Then we'll both devote our attention to the problem," he said, reaching for her hand. "After this dance.

"You know, Morna," he said as they moved around the floor, "I think we could get on very well. I'm not nearly the rogue everyone thinks I am, you know. If the right girl came along I could settle down happily."

When Ted took her home he stopped the car outside her flat. His arm went round her shoulders, and he pulled her towards him. She wasn't sure that she wanted to resist as he kissed her.

Some children can drop off to sleep quickly and easily.

Others seem to find it impossible.

thelwell's
BRAT RACE
THINGS THAT GO BUMP IN THE NIGHT

Try letting them take a few of their favourite toys to bed —

— Or take them into your own bed occasionally — it will do them no harm.

She seemed to hang for an age between heaven and earth, then suddenly alarm bells were ringing.

Only wolves, or foxes, kissed like that!

"That's enough!" she said and smiled, still reeling from his kiss.

"Go on, admit it, you'd no intention of settling down, had you?" she added. "That was just a little act to put me off my guard."

"Could be."

Morna couldn't help laughing as she got out of the car. She was picturing a chicken being chased along a country lane by a smart, well-dressed fox.

"What's so funny?" Ted demanded.

"You've just given me an idea for the competition. Thanks, Ted," she said as he started the engine. "A girl needs a night out like that once or twice in a lifetime. It was wonderful."

ABOUT a week later, Morna was busy in the children's window of Carter's. She was arranging a little scene which showed an extremely smart fox chasing a chicken along a woodland path. Looking on were the usual woodland creatures — squirrels, rabbits, owls and blue-tits.

But stepping forward to do battle with the fox was a handsome St Bernard dog.

Suddenly, she was aware of someone watching her, and when she turned she saw Nicholas Haddow on the street outside.

He grinned at her and she waved happily. He came inside the store and joined her in the window.

"Congratulations! You got my letter saying you'd won?" he said. "Very clever display of yours, Morna."

"Thanks, Nick. I was delighted to win," she said. "It was an idea I got when I was on a date."

"Ah yes, a fox chasing a chicken. I wonder why?"

"Well, it's really Ted and me." She laughed.

"Yes, but what's the significance of the St Bernard?"

"Oh, that's my secret," Morna said. "But I might tell you some day."

"You're not serious about Ted then?" he asked carefully. "I mean . . ."

"I never was serious."

He smiled. "Then how would you like to come out with me this evening to celebrate your win?"

"I'd love to," she replied.

"Good," Nick said happily. "How about some coffee to keep you going until then?"

He took her arm and led her towards the door at the back of the shop window, and as she went out, Morna looked back for a moment and smiled happily — at the fox, the chicken . . . and the St Bernard.

——————— * **THE END** * ———————

Complete Story
by EMMA CLARE

W E'LL be late, Mummy, we'll be late!"

Amy hops impatiently from one foot to the other, hindering my attempts to coax her unwilling hair into bunches.

"Hurry!" she urges me again.

Does a tie go left over right, or right over left? I wonder. Round once, or twice? I try to recall my own school-tie days, but eventually give up and

"I'LL BE WAITING"

Always remember — it's never too late to keep a promise.

transfer her to the more experienced hands of her father.

"*You* aren't going to be late, young lady, but *I* certainly am!" Edward tells her as he slips the ends of her tie into the front of her pinafore dress.

Ready at last, our pint-sized daughter parades in front of us and I watch my own mixed feelings of pride and regret reflected in Edward's face.

Regret for the baby we are inevitably losing, and pride for the independent little individual she has become.

She seems such a tiny scrap as she skips off down the path to wait for me at the gate.

"You're supposed to be feeling relieved today," Edward reminds me, as I gaze thoughtfully out of the window." "It's only possessive mothers who cry when their children start school."

"I'm not going to cry," I assure him, sounding far more certain than I actually feel. "It's just that she doesn't look old enough to be going to school."

We both look out at Amy, sitting on the gate, her baby-fine hair already escaping its restricting ribbons.

Edward sighs. "No. You're right, she doesn't."

"You should be reassuring me," I remind him, and we laugh at ourselves as he goes to answer the telephone.

I rap on the window to attract Amy's attention and, again, she calls out that we shall be late.

"It was the hospital," Edward says with a smile as he replaces the receiver. "Sara Gleeson had a baby boy lat night. They're both fine."

I can see the delight in his eyes and I share it with him.

Even after 20 years as a busy GP in our small town, Edward never fails to get a thrill from the safe arrival of a healthy, much-wanted baby. Especially when, as in this case, it follows long years of waiting.

Maybe it is because Edward and I know all about the waiting and hoping, and the disappointments from our own experience.

We'd been married 14 years before Amy finally arrived. Now, after such a long wait, five years doesn't seem very long to have had her to ourselves.

Whatever my own misgivings, I am determined to match Amy's enthusiasm, and her excited chatter carries us both along through the familiar streets to Fensdown Primary School.

It is only as we enter the large, bright classroom, and a sea of inquisitive faces turns towards us, that the small hand tightens its hold on mine.

"You will come back soon, won't you, Mummy?" a strained little voice pleads as I prepare to abandon her to a room full of strangrs.

"Very soon!" I promise, and close the door firmly behind me.

Her question strikes like an echo from the past. I can almost hear myself uttering the same words to my father as he prepared to leave me at this door so long ago.

A bright anorak hangs on the peg where my old green cape used to hang, and I remember how I buried my face in it and cried when he had said his goodbyes and gone.

"YOU will come back soon, won't you?" I begged him. It wasn't that I minded being left at school. I was used to it by that time. It was just that I had no idea how long he'd be gone, and it felt like forever.

No-one had said he'd be back in a week, or a month, as they did when people went on holiday, or into hospital. I was only told he had to go. And the way they'd said it had worried me.

Taking my cold hands in his, he stooped down in front of me so that his gentle grey eyes were level with mine. There was no evidence of his own heartache and uncertainty as he promised me that he would be back soon.

"Hey, come on, Maureen, you're made of tougher stuff than that!" he told me, as I bit back the threatening tears. "Why, this old war will be over in a few months and then I'll be back home again."

I believed him, maybe he even believed himself, when he led me to the open door.

"See over there?" he said, pointing to the green gates of the school yard. "One of these days when you come out of this door, I'll be waiting there for you. You'll see."

He bent to kiss the top of my head while I stared fixedly in front of me. Then he strode away without a backward glance at the little girl watching him go.

I watched until tears distorted my view of his straight figure. I ran back across the porch and sank my face into the material of my coat.

"Has your dad got to go?" someone asked matter-of-factly, and I nodded desperately, without looking up.

"Where to?"

"France," I sobbed, wishing the voice with its unfamiliar accent would go away.

"That's not far!" it informed me knowledgeably. "Mine's in Jerusalem!"

At this important-sounding piece of information, I recovered sufficiently to look up at the red-haired boy beside me, his small chin jutting out proudly.

"He's with the Argyll and Sutherlands. Who's your dad with?"

"I — I don't know," I stammered. "It's the Army, though."

Ginger McAlister looked down his freckled nose at my ignorance and ran to join the others as the clanging bell echoed through the building.

I followed, trying to console myself with my father's words. *This old war will be over in a few months!*

But to a little girl who had never spent one day of her short life away from him, a few months was a lifetime.

I pulled my cardigan sleeve over my hand and scrubbed hard at my tear-streaked face as the teacher's concerned gaze sought me out.

"What is it, Maureen?"

I shook my head, refusing to explain, sure that everyone would laugh at me for being such a baby. After all, I wasn't the only one.

"She's not feeling well." Ginger's voice spoke up without hesitation, and I smiled a watery smile of thanks.

It was Ginger who accompanied me to the porch to fetch a drink. He promised he would tell no-one the real reason I was crying, and from then on, I was his constant shadow.

A T break-times, I spread my green cape on the ground so that we could sit on it while I plied him with jam sandwiches and questions.

When an aeroplane droned overhead, he would shade his eyes with his hands and peer upwards before issuing his nochalant verdict.

"One of ours!"

War barely touched our sleepy town and our practice trips to the air-raid shelter were simply a welcome break from routine for us.

"I'm going to be a soldier when I grow up," Ginger informed me one day, as we followed the crocodile of children back from the shelter.

"And you will marry me as well?" I asked hopefully.

He shook his head emphatically, his face full of scorn. "I'm going to marry Shirley Temple!"

"She's stupid!" I told him sulkily.

"She is not!" he objected. "She's got curls. Your hair's all spiky!"

I licked my fingers and indignantly pressed my fine fringe into place.

"I wouldn't want to marry you anyway!" I retaliated. "You talk funny — and your dad wears a skirt!"

"He does not!" He looked outraged as he clenched and unclenched his fists. "It's a kilt. You don't even know who your dad's with!"

After that he made a point of ignoring me and I pretended not to care.

I pretended not to miss his stories about the castle in Scotland, where he had lived before he and his mother came to stay with his grandparents. It didn't matter that it gained one more turret, or another dungeon, with every story. I believed every word!

Then one morning, after prayers, the headmistress told us all that Ginger wouldn't be coming back to school for a few days. And, when he did, we must all be especially nice to him.

"His father has been killed in action," she told us sadly.

I wasn't really sure what action meant, but thought it must be another place, like Jerusalem, or France.

But the thought of Ginger's father never coming back to his castle again struck chill at my heart. I pictured the beloved face of my own father which never appeared at the school gate however often I looked for it.

136

A SURPRISINGLY normal Ginger was back at school a few days later, helping to sort the proceeds of our "Rubber Appeal" with as much excitement as the rest of us.

In a corner of the classroom, the pile of rubber balls, inner-tubes and hot-water bottles soon reached gigantic proportions, or so it seemed. And Ginger had to stand on a chair so that he could sit his own blue teddy-bear hot-water bottle in pride of place on the top.

"We must all give what we can," the teacher reminded us as she held out a hand to help him down.

I noticed that she still kept his hand in hers as she thanked us all for giving so generously. Somehow, she looked strangely sad.

Ginger just stood and stared at his teddy-bottle, and I wondered if he was wishing he hadn't given it away after all.

At break-time I spread my cape on the ground and he sat down on it without a word.

"I won't tell anyone you've been crying," I promised, as he dragged grubby hands down his wet cheeks.

"You could get your teddy-bottle back again." I tried to console him.

But he shook his head, brushing the last of his tears away with his sleeve.

"Everybody must give what they can," he insisted bravely.

As if that small boy hadn't given enough . . .

I thought of the card Ginger's father had sent to him at Christmas. There had been a picture of Bethlehem on the front and the words "From The Holy Land."

To me, Bethlehem conjured up a picture of a baby in a stable, and all the magic that was Christmas, not of a place which robbed a little boy of his father.

But however much I shared in Ginger's grief, it was nothing to the blow which fell for me a few months later.

I don't remember my mother telling me what was printed on the flimsy sheet of paper as she crushed it in her hand. I only remembered her heartbroken refusal to accept that the man she loved was missing.

At least he hadn't been killed in action, I consoled myself. Missing wasn't so bad. Lots of things went missing and were found again.

And, just as my mother refused to believe the worst, I refused to stop looking hopefully towards the school gate whenever I ran out into the yard.

I WAS 11 when victory brought its riotous programme of parties and parades to the flag-draped streets.

To a colour-starved child, the brilliant confusion of noise and laughter was too much to resist. And enough to make me forget, for a while, that I hadn't as much to celebrate as some.

As dusk fell, I sat on a wall and watched the procession of servicemen marching down the centre of the road, while they sang the well-loved songs.

Scanning the khaki uniforms, I told myself that I must surely see the face I was searching for — the face of my father. But I didn't. And suddenly it seemed a hollow victory.

The sound of bagpipes heralded the arrival of the Scottish soldiers, magnificent in their dress uniforms. It was then that I spotted Ginger, standing white-faced and proud on the opposite side of the street.

Darting between the figures in their swinging kilts, I followed him as he turned down one of the side streets leading to the canal.

For a long time we didn't speak, but sat on the tow-path and stared into the murky depths, listening to the sounds of dancing in the streets.

"I don't think I'll be a soldier," Ginger said suddenly.

I was so glad. "Won't you marry Shirley Temple either?" I teased.

He glared at me for reminding him of his foolishness, and sent a stick skimming across the water to hide his embarrassment.

"All those stupid curls!" he scoffed, rubbing his shoe backwards and forwards in the dust. "Anyway, I like you better," he mumbled without looking up.

I sprang to my feet as he began walking back the way we'd come.

"I do really like the way you talk, Ginger," I assured him. "And I thought the Scottish soldiers looked the best."

This time he did look up, grinning all over his freckled face, and I slipped my hand in his as we made our way home.

A few weeks later I left Fensdown Primary for the last time and, after the long summer holidays, took my place at the Girls' High School.

Gradually, amongst all the excitement of settling into a new way of life, I began to accept that, like Ginger, I had been one of the unlucky ones.

I think even Mother began to accept it, too, but with her acceptance some small spark of life seemed to go out of her.

It was as if her constant hoping had kept it alive. When hope had died, something deep within her had died too.

Nothing could possibly have prepared us for the staggering shock of seeing my father walk into the house one day, as calmly as though he'd just been down to the shops.

Afterwards, I could never remember much about those first few minutes. There were explanations about an injury and loss of memory. But mostly it was a confusion of tears and laughter, and for me, a bewildering sense of disappointment.

Miraculously, he still looked almost the same as the man who had left us all those years ago. He sounded the same, he even laughed the same. But he felt like a stranger.

At night he came up and sat on the side of my bed, just as he'd always done before. But our conversation was forced as we both tried too hard.

I longed to ask him if he still remembered what he'd said about waiting at the school gate, but I never did. I didn't want to know if he'd forgotten.

I pretended not to notice the tears on my hair when he leaned over to kiss me goodnight.

And long after he'd gone downstairs, I was still asking myself why, when he had said his goodbyes so cheerfully, should he cry when it was all over and we were together again?

What made a man, who had had to be brave in order to survive, sad enough to cry? Was I a disappointment to him after all this time?

My young mind never did sort out the answers, and by the time I was old enough, I suppose I'd forgotten the questions.

Until today, when they are suddenly as clear as if it were only last week. And now, at last, I can understand.

He had gone away leaving a child who was no bigger than Amy. He'd returned to find a stranger, who was rapidly leaving childhood behind.

His tears were for the part of me he'd missed, those precious years that we should have shared, and didn't.

I TAKE my time in the morning sunshine so as to avoid the cluster of mothers chatting at the gate. Another morning I may join them, but not today.

I had said to Edward earlier that I wouldn't cry, but now, as I make my lonely way across the deserted playground my vision blurs.

"Hey, come on. You're made of tougher stuff than that!"

I look up at the well-remembered words.

He doesn't look so different. Older, of course, and more lined. But the grey eyes are still as gentle, and his back almost as straight as when he said those words so long ago.

Self-consciously, I take the handkerchief he offers.

"What are you doing out this early?" I ask him ungraciously, and slip my arm through his so he knows I don't mean it that way.

"Didn't I say I'd be waiting here one of these days?" He smiles the slow, comforting smile I've known all my life, and I wonder if he really knows just how much he means to me.

I doubt it, just as Amy will probably never know how much the next five years of her life will mean to her grandfather.

"Well, what did our little Ginger think of school then?" he asks, and laughs at my disapproval of the dreaded nickname.

"All right," he obliges. "Amy! But it won't be long before she's Ginger to everyone, just like her dad. And it didn't do him much harm, did it?"

I know he's right. With her flaming head of hair, Amy is just like her father.

To those who only know the compassionate, understanding man who is my husband, Edward is simply Dr McAlister.

But to the few who still remember the staunch little boy who gave so much, he will always be Ginger.

——————— * **THE END** * ———————

WHAT

A cantankerous uncle,
three boisterous children,
a smallholding full of animals
and the most infuriating
"helper" she'd ever met.
Find out for yourselves . . .

KATIE DID NEXT

KATIE stared at the local paper, propped against the marmalade pot where her Uncle Henry had left it. There was a smear of marmalade right across the headline and she suppressed an urge to scream.

Every morning it had happened, ever since she'd arrived, and every morning she'd managed to hold back angry words. She snatched up the paper, wiped off the marmalade, then stood by the kitchen sink, reading a squared-off advertisement in one corner.

Overworked? Need A Helping Hand? Desperate?

If you are, contact us for help!

There was a telephone number, and without a second thought, Katie went to the hall, unstuck a toffee from the telephone receiver, and dialled it. It shrilled three times, then was picked up. Before she could stop herself she'd blurted out her woes.

"I'm overworked! I need a helping hand, and I'm desperate!"

The man's voice was wearily amused. "So is everyone who phones us. What can we do for you?"

"Whatever it is you do to help other overworked mums! I'm not

Complete Story by ELIZABETH ASHCROFT

one but I've got an aged and obstinate uncle, twins and a rebelling teenager, and a smallholding to run. It's the school holidays and Uncle Henry has just announced he's going on a package tour and won't be able to help with the tomatoes!

"And," she added for good measure, "a Siamese cat who keeps disappearing!"

The voice began to sound interested.

"You've got troubles all right. But what exactly is it you want? A child minder, an uncle watcher, a tomato picker, or a cat catcher?"

He sounded, Katie thought, highly amused at her plight.

"I need someone who can help me," she said coldly. "Someone who doesn't mind working hard! Which is more than I bet you do, sitting there answering the phone all day!"

She wasn't usually rude to people, but she'd just about had enough.

"Here, hold on!" The voice sounded indignant. "There's no need to take it out on me. We're short staffed. All the mums are feeling the combined effects of school holidays and the heatwave. And I'm afraid we're fully booked up."

"You haven't got *anyone*?" Katie wailed despairingly.

Through the open door she could see Ben and Babsie chasing the hens in the run. There was a terrible squawking and flapping of wings, then Babsie tripped and lay howling.

"I've told you before not to chase the chickens!" she yelled. "They won't lay if you frighten them! Come out at once!"

The voice on the other end of the phone sounded puzzled. "Chickens? You want someone who knows about chickens as well?"

"No!" she snapped. "I don't care who comes, just send someone, *please*!"

He sounded mildly reproving. "We always do our best. There may be a cancellation. Maybe Miss Phipps can come along."

Katie gave him her address and put the phone down with exaggerated calm. God bless Miss Phipps, if only she'd come — quickly.

She went back to the pile of washing-up, thinking of where she should be right now — on holiday with Alan at his home instead of here. She remembered his horrified expression when she'd told him she couldn't go away with him after all.

"Look after your Uncle Henry?" he'd queried in surprise.

She'd nodded miserably. She'd known Alan for six months, since he joined the executive ranks of the advertising agency where she worked.

He was handsome, knew all the best places and drove a low-slung sports car. She'd never met anyone like him before and had been swept off her usually firm feet.

Troubles in her family, she reflected mournfully, never seemed to come singly. First, her sister was rushed to hospital with appendicitis, and the three children had been packed off to Uncle Henry's for what her mother called "a month in the sun."

Then Uncle Henry had a row with his housekeeper, Miss Smith, who departed in a huff, and Penelope, the twins' elder sister, had fallen down some steps in the barn and broken an ankle. Consequently she couldn't do a thing to help Uncle Henry with the twins, who were six.

In a panic, he'd phoned Katie's mother.

"Not to worry, Henry," she'd trilled down the phone. "Katie is home for a while. She'll come down and help out."

"*Me?*" Katie had stared aghast at her mother. "But I'm going to Alan's! He wants me to meet his people!"

And be looked over, she thought. They want to see if I'm suitable for him.

"I can't go to look after Uncle Henry now, of all times!" she'd protested.

Katie's mother had surveyed her calmly. "He's in trouble, dear, and no-one else can go. He is *family*, after all."

Katie sighed. To her mother, the family came before anything.

"But I'm going to Alan's on Saturday! I'm all packed. He'll never speak to me again!"

"Oh, don't be silly, dear, of course he will," her mother had said. "This is an emergency, after all. And if you're all packed it will save you time in the morning. I told Henry you'd be there tomorrow."

"Oh, Mum!" Katie had protested, but she couldn't get out of it. And Uncle Henry had been marvellous to her, helping out with her Art School grant.

So she'd sat through a despairingly fraught meal with Alan and watched his eyes grown cool across the candlelit table.

Coldly, he'd said he supposed she'd write to him.

"Oh, of course I will! And you can always come down to visit me!"

"Me?" He'd looked horrified. "Can you see me ploughing round a farm, feeding chickens and spreading dung?"

She couldn't.

And so she'd arrived at Sleepydown Farm just in time to pull Babsie from the pond.

Babsie had spluttered, then a wide beam had spread across her angelic face.

"Auntie Katie! Oh, it's super you've come! Now it'll be fun! We haven't had any fun yet."

FUN, Katie thought grimly now as she turned from the washing-up. If mountains of dishes, cooking enormous meals three times a day, keeping the twins out of trouble, trying to find George, the cat, and in her spare time feeding hens and picking tomatoes — if all that was *fun*, then she was having a whale of a time!

And Uncle Henry, for the first time she could remember, had been grumpy. He'd spent his days pacing through the house or working like mad in the long greenhouses.

"Have you seen Uncle Henry?" she asked Penelope, who was sitting comfortably in the kitchen rocking-chair, her ankle in plaster.

Continued on page 147

LOST,

Those were the options Sami gave when she vanished in a strange city — but her ability to make friends stood her in good stead . . .

By
**ROSEMARY
ALEXANDER**

YOU'RE not going to believe this but, cross my heart, every word is true, and I'd be grateful to hear from anyone who could offer an explanation.

Sami, a lean, keen animal positively bursting with energy, was nine months old when she came to live with me. Daughter of a wild, aristocratic Lurcher and a gentle Springer spaniel, she inherited her zest, agility, and whiskery chin from her father, whilst her glossy, black and tan coat, and her loving

nature, came from the maternal side of the family.

The previous owner had taken her back to the breeder because he claimed she was untrainable, a completely unwarranted slur on her character.

When we met, she placed a huge paw on my arm, and laid her head in my lap, in a charmingly submissive gesture. She might have faults — who hasn't — but an affectionate dog does its best to please.

STOLEN OR STRAYED?

"Are you sure you can manage her?" the breeder inquired, rather guiltily, as though aware she'd fostered a potential criminal.

"Perfectly sure," I answered, without a qualm, leading Sami off to her new home.

To show her appreciation of my domestic arrangements, the moment I released her, she raced into the dining-room, leapt through the service hatch into the kitchen, bounded upstairs with the speed of an express train, vaulted every bed, then hurtled down to the sitting-room.

We had a serious chat. I warned her this was not the kind of behaviour I tolerated from members of my household, and showed her the chair reserved for her own use.

The performance was not repeated. Oh, Sami wasn't an angel. During the first 24 hours, she chewed up a pair of gardening shoes, and stole a loaf of bread from the draining-board, but she looked suitably humble when I pointed out the error of her ways. She didn't always respond immediately I called her, but hounds of any sort are individualists — which is why I like the breed.

I took her to training classes, and the whole thing was a complete fiasco. The presence of 20 other dogs excited her too much to pay attention to her lessons. But we understood each other and, by the end of six weeks, had established a mutal rapport.

WITHOUT doubt, Sami is highly intelligent. If I'm out, when the postman calls, she picks up the letters, and places them neatly beside the chair at my desk ready to be answered.

She can distinguish Saturday from the rest of the week, because a friend always calls at 9 a.m. to accompany us on a walk. Only on Saturdays does she wait at the front door from 8.55 a.m. until the bell rings.

Within days, she had learned my routine, and adapted her own to fit into the programme.

At the end of the second month, I had to make a business trip to Leicester, and decided to take her with me. A fresh environment would test exactly how far our relationship had progressed.

If she observed the proprieties amongst strangers, I could honestly claim to be able to take her anywhere. She would be the trust-worthy companion I had known she could be at our initial encounter.

The journey was a nightmare. The skies opened to let loose torrential rain. Thunder hammered on the roof of the car, and heavy lorries turned the motorway into a surging ocean.

Curled up on the rear seat, Sami slept, with only an occasional twitch of the ears to show she noticed the minor discomforts, and she did nothing to distract my attention from the job in hand. In short, she passed the first stage of the test with flying colours.

K

We arrived in good time, with over an hour to spare before my 3 p.m. appointment, so I took her into a park. Sweeping acres of grass allowed travel-weary legs to be stretched to the limit. Clumps of trees held the enthralling prospect of a rabbit.

Enjoying her reward for patience during a long, tedious journey, Sami raced in wide circles, as though attached to me by an invisible hundred-yard wire, gloriously free but careful to keep me within sight.

No tremor of fear disturbed me, as I ambled placidly in her wake. (I didn't know that, the following day, she was due to come in season, or I wouldn't have been so complacent.) Other dogs joined in the fun, but this didn't worry me in the slightest.

Sami makes friends with everyone, and enjoys showing off her acrobatic skills, including the vertical take-off which is her speciality. If she hadn't already possessed a name, when I found her, I'd have called her Harriet. No jump-jet ever rose straight into the air from a standing start with greater ease.

So there she was, chasing around, happy as a pig in clover but a good deal more lively, whilst I smiled idiotically at her antics. One circular sweep took her into a copse, with half a dozen companions in hot pursuit, and I waited confidently for the lithe, red-collared figure to streak back towards me.

The confidence was misplaced. I waited — and waited. The copse was suddenly still and empty. I called, and called again. Nothing happened.

Apparently, she and her train of companions had vanished into the hillside, like the Pied Piper of Hamelin and his train of rats.

A cold shiver of apprehension chilled me. Yet again I called and whistled, but the invisible wire had broken.

I went back to the car. Surely that was the spot she'd make for, if she'd lost her bearings? Never before had she left me for more than a few seconds. I couldn't understand what had caused the unaccountable lapse.

Half an hour passed. The business that had brought me to Leicester would have to be postponed indefinitely.

I explained my plight to the park keeper, who didn't regard it as a drama. Looking out for lost dogs obviously took up a large part of his working day.

Fellow dog-owners were more sympathetic. One girl even drove round the perimeter of the park on the lookout for a streak of greased lightning wearing a red collar, but there was no sign of Sami.

My spirits hit rock bottom. Dreadful pictures flashed through my brain. She was lost in a vast city, amidst streets seething with traffic. The motorway's sinister drone must be less than a mile away. Why, oh why, had I ever allowed her off the lead?

WHEN she'd been missing for an hour, I steeled myself to face a lonely journey home, and went in search of the nearest police station. I might never see her again, but the sight of a blue uniform would provide a measure of reassurance.

The sergeant behind the counter greeted me cheerfully.

I confessed, "I've lost a black and tan lurcher, with a red collar."

"And a whiskery chin?"

Astonishment struck me dumb, for a moment. I know our policemen are wonderful, but I hadn't expected them to have clairvoyant powers?

"Yes, with a beard like Abraham Lincoln. She ran off in the park, and I'm frantic with worry. She's never been to Leicester before. We live a hundred and fifty miles from here. She couldn't possibly find her way home."

"Well, she won't need to try. She walked in through the door a few minutes ago, and went up to the canteen. Whilst we're talking, two burly detectives are doing their best to catch her."

I said you wouldn't believe it, but that's exactly what happened. On her own, without human assistance, Sami had picked exactly the right spot to end her wandering.

The detectives succeeded in capturing her and, I'm glad to say, she must have resisted her admirers' attempts to chat her up. There were no disastrous consequences of her romp through the woods.

I realise girls will be girls, and puppies can be adorable, but eight little Samis would strain the resources of the most ardent animal lover.

I still puzzle over the mystery of why she made a bee-line for one particular building in a completely unknown city. My parents taught me to ask a policeman, if I was lost, but I hadn't passed on this vital information to Sami.

David Attenborough, or some learned professor who has spent years researching into animal behaviour, may know the answer. I'm utterly baffled. Perhaps it was the delicious aroma from the canteen that eventually provided a happy ending to this story! ∎

Continued from page 143

"He's outside, I think. If you ask me, he's missing old Miss Smith. *I* think he's in love with her!"

"Don't gossip. And make yourself useful."

Penelope's dark blue eyes flashed indignantly.

"I'm sick," she said defensively.

"Just because you've broken your ankle, doesn't mean you can't peel potatoes," Katie said firmly.

She'd had enough of Penelope's airs and graces after only three days. But all that had paled into relative insignificance when Uncle Henry dropped his bombshell at breakfast, half an hour ago . . .

"You can cope next week, can't you, Katie? I'm going away for a few days."

Katie had nearly dropped the frying-pan.

"Going away? But you can't! What about the tomatoes and the twins, and that wretched cat!"

Uncle Henry had surveyed her mildly over his toast and marmalade.

"I'm going on a package tour," he announced, with determination. "To Spain for a week."

"Spain?" Her voice had risen to an anguished wail. "What ever for?"

"It's time I saw a bit of the world. I'm getting old. Soon be too old to enjoy it."

"But not right at this minute. Not when you're really busy! And

I'm here on my own!"

Uncle Henry had smiled, almost his old smile. "And coping very well, Katie dear. Wouldn't suggest it if I didn't think you could do it. I'll get someone in to help with the tomatoes, never fear."

And he was going. Just like that. In two days' time!

THE next morning, Katie was nearly in tears. The toaster went up in flames and Ben let the hens out. And the washing-machine flooded the kitchen. Then someone banged on the back door.

"Who is it?" she shouted, mopping the floor.

"Me," a calm voice said.

And in walked a tall, tanned man, wearing a smart suit. He had a small case under one arm.

Katie, paddling across the kitchen barefoot, jeans rolled up to her knees, blinked. He looked like someone from another world, the world she used to know in the art designer's room where she worked.

He coughed gently. "Are you still overworked . . . er, desperate?"

For the first time since she'd arrived here, hope tinged her voice. "Desperate? The Agency! You've got someone for me? Have you brought Miss Phipps?"

"Afraid not." He shook his head, looking in mild amazement at her bedraggled appearance. "But if you're really in trouble I've come to lend you a hand. All right?"

"You?" She gazed at him unbelievingly. He didn't look as though he knew one end of a can-opener from another. He looked, she thought wistfully, a little like Alan.

"Me." He unlocked his case and pulled out some clothes. "If there's somewhere I can change?"

She gestured feebly to the downstairs cloakroom. "Through there."

He appeared five minutes later. His jeans were faded and the striped T-shirt too small, but he took over.

"Newspaper, bucket, mop," he demanded, and Katie thrust them at him.

In half an hour the kitchen was cleared. The machine, to her astonishment, was mended and working away happily in the corner once more.

"Well, that's something," she conceded grudgingly.

He shot a glance at her. He looked, she thought triumphantly, a little bedraggled, with splotches of water all over his jeans.

"It'll go on the bill, don't worry," he said. "What now?"

"Well, I haven't made the beds yet, or done the vegetables. And the hens have to be fed and the cat's disappeared again. And coffee for Uncle Henry in his greenhouse — want me to go on?"

He looked at her grimly.

"You," he said blandly, "can make the beds. I'll do the coffee and the cooking."

"And who's the employer round here, anyway?" Katie demanded indignantly.

"Want me to go?" he asked, and she caved in weakly.

148

"AND I QUOTE . . ."

Pam Ayres made a reputation reciting her unusual humorous verses on TV, in her own inimitable rural accent. They have also proved popular on LPs. Her first published collection was *Some of Me Poems* (1976).

I wish I was a pop star,
Colourful and brash,
With me earoles full of crotchets
And me wallet full of cash.

What other single comment
Causes panic and despair
Like someone saying, "Keep still!
There's a wasp caught in your hair!"

"If you're doing lunch, it's chops. In the fridge. And Uncle Henry has coffee at eleven."

She glanced out of the window later and saw him taking a tray into the greenhouse. Ten minutes later he still hadn't come back.

She stamped over to the greenhouse and found him sitting in a wheelbarrow, chatting companionably with Uncle Henry, who raised his bushy eyebrows at her.

"Katie, you didn't tell me you'd asked a friend round. So nice for her to have someone her own age about, Charles," he added, and Katie realised she hadn't known his name until now.

"Friend?" she repeated blankly, and Charles unwound his long legs and got up.

"Your uncle's been telling me about Spain. Fantastic place, Spain." And he took her arm and led her past tomato plants outside.

"He thinks you're the cat's whiskers, managing so well," he said dryly. "So I told him I'd just dropped in. No need to let him know you're paying, specially if he's off tomorrow."

His unexpected understanding startled her. Then he touched his forehead and gave a mock bow.

"Waiting for orders, ma'am."

Suddenly she thought he was the most unsettling man she'd ever met. "You can clean out the chicken run. And then the twins will have to have a good wash before lunch. They're in the barn."

149

That should keep him happy, she thought vindictively.

Surprisingly, the twins came without a murmur, and Penelope gazed adoringly at him, hobbling along hanging on to his arm. And he'd turned the chops into a fantastic casserole, which she'd never had time to do.

By mid-afternoon, Uncle Henry was calling him Charlie, and Penelope was in the throes of an adolescent crush.

Charles had found the cat hidden in Uncle Henry's wardrobe, and George, to Katie's surprise, didn't even scratch him.

By now she was simmering with barely suppressed rage. He'd even helped Uncle Henry pack his bags and recommended a certain restaurant near the harbour.

Uncle Henry, Katie decided, was behaving in a decidedly odd manner. He'd never been farther than Brighton in his life, and here he was jetting off to Spain at a moment's notice.

Suddenly she remembered the greenhouses.

"Uncle Henry! You've arranged for the help tomorrow?"

He peered at her over the tea and cake Charles had brought out on to the overgrown lawn.

"Of course. Old Bob from the village and his nephew. Not to worry."

Charles sat on a creaking deckchair then caught her disapproving eye.

"Oh, well," he said, getting up again. "Better get on with the lawn. Needs mowing."

He ambled away to the shed and pushed out the enormous, old-fashioned machine.

"It doesn't work," Katie informed him with pleasure.

"It doesn't?" He promptly took it to pieces with Ben's delighted assistance, and in an hour was cutting the lawn. He looked, Katie thought crossly, as though he owned the place.

Uncle Henry looked at her curiously.

"Nice chap," he observed. "But you don't seem to care for him. Does that Alan get in the way? Never met him yet."

Katie flushed. She couldn't tell Uncle Henry that Alan hated the country, only set foot in it under voluble protest. She stared at the wide expanse of blue sky and smelled the newly-cut grass.

A picture flashed into her mind of hot and dusty city streets, and scurrying, bad-tempered crowds. And suddenly, to her astonishment, she knew she didn't want to go back.

She lay back on the warm grass, and was just dozing off when Charles loomed over her.

He held the shears in his brown hands, and handed them to her.

"The edges need cutting," he announced, and she blinked at him. "We all can't fall asleep, you know," he added with a grin.

Silently fuming, she took the shears.

Just wait till tomorrow, she thought, when Uncle Henry's gone. She'd think of all the worst jobs for him. Clean out the hens, clean the oven, wash the kitchen floor. But then she realised he did them all, efficiently — and came back for more.

SHE was struggling in the greenhouse, facing long rows of ripe early tomatoes. Old Bob had turned up, complaining of a bad back, and taken himself off home again, leaving his nephew, Len.

Katie crawled along between the rows, picking the ripe fruit. Perspiration dripped down her forehead, her legs and knees ached horribly.

Then, behind her, she heard a polite cough. It was Charles.

"I must say," he said kindly, "you really do look a bit desperate now. Like me to help?"

"No thanks!" She glowered up at him through tendrils of damp hair. "You can — oh, you can do the ironing. There's a pile of it!"

When, finally, she staggered into the kitchen, he made tea and poured it out for her.

Ben and Babsie were sitting quietly watching television while Penelope helped Charles make sandwiches.

"Penelope!" Katie said sharply. "That's not your job!"

"It's not Charlie's either!" Penelope scowled. "It's not a *man's* job!"

"Oh yes it is, if he gets paid for it!" Katie said unwisely. "And don't call him Charlie!"

Penelope's eyes widened in surprise. "I thought there was something funny going on! You're *paying* Charlie? Imagine having to pay to have a boyfriend!"

Katie went bright pink and Charles laughed.

"It's not that at all," Katie began, and Charles butted in.

"It's my job, Penelope. I help overworked mums and dads. It's an Agency which helps people in trouble. Poor old Katie was in trouble, so I'm helping her out. And most people call me Charlie," he added.

Katie realised belatedly that she never called him anything at all.

Penelope turned adoring eyes to Charles. She looked smug.

"Katie's not anybody's mum, and I wouldn't say she was ever desperate," Penelope said. "Uncle Henry thinks she's very capable. She's got a smashing job in London."

"London." His voice was flat. "Big place, London. I'd rather live here, myself, where you can breathe."

"Oh, so would I," Penelope murmured.

Charles glanced at his watch. "Well, that's it. Clocking-off time."

Katie felt oddly deflated. Then she shook herself. She'd wash her hair and have a long soak with lots of bubble bath. And relax, when the twins were in bed.

"Can't you stay a bit longer?" Penelope implored.

Charles smiled down at her. "Sorry, love. Got to go. Desk work."

★　　　★　　　★　　　★

On the Monday morning, neither old Bob nor his nephew appeared, and Ben came out in a suspicious-looking rash. By noon it was worse.

The doctor diagnosed measles, cheerfully stating that Babsie would probably get it, too.

Katie gave a despairing sigh. She might have known it. Grimly she got through the chores, picked tomatoes, roped in Penelope to look after Ben, and waited for Charles to appear.

But he didn't. Not till after lunch, when she was almost in tears from sheer weariness.

"Where have you been?" she demanded as he wandered into the kitchen.

"Working," he said blandly. "There's a lot of paperwork to catch up on. Don't forget this is a special job, helping you out. We're still short-staffed, and Miss Phipps has resigned."

"Well, are you here to work or just to prop up the doorway?"

He grinned lazily. "Waiting for orders, ma'am."

"The whole greenhouse has to be gone over for ripe tomatoes, picked, graded, and boxed," she informed him coldly. "So you can make a start. I'll join you shortly."

He turned at the door. "Where's the glamorous Penelope, and the twins?"

"Ben has measles and Penelope is looking after him and waiting for Babsie's spots to appear."

For once he looked nonplussed, she was pleased to see.

They were still working in the greenhouse at six o'clock that evening.

Charles sat back on his heels, dusty and dishevelled.

"Overtime after five o'clock," he announced, and she rubbed a grubby hand tiredly over her forehead.

"You look tired," he said.

"I do?" She looked at him through the leafy fronds of tomato plants, and suddenly found herself smiling at him. An odd sort of companionship had grown up between them during the long afternoon.

"I am tired, dead tired. I'd like to fall into a bath and be taken out to a meal, and not have to cook it."

He grinned. "I'll cook tea for the kids while you're in the bath," he offered.

Suddenly it was one of the best ideas she'd heard for years.

"Treble overtime?" she queried, and then to her astonishment he leaned forward and kissed her gently on the nose.

"No charge," he said, and suddenly a tall shadow loomed over them.

"Kate! What on earth do you think you're doing?"

SHE looked up — straight into Alan's furious blue eyes. Immaculate as ever, he looked completely out of place in Uncle Henry's greenhouse.

"Alan!" she stammered, getting awkwardly to her feet. Her back ached, her knees ached, and her head ached from the stifling heat.

Continued on page 154

Yes, we know — you've missed having a crossword! Well, here you are — go to it, you happy puzzlers!

Clues Across.

3. Fragment — often found in the horse's mouth? (3)
8. When you're like this you might have measles (6)
9. Parade that often finds the culprit (8)
10. Musical composed by two American soldiers? (4)
11. Girl I love anyhow (5)
12. Principal water supply? (4)
13. Fire-side footwear — or banana skins? (8)
14. Hired at a flat rate (6)
16. Inseparable companions — or ghosts (7)
18. Told how the family are kept together? (7)
21. Female relative (6)
24. Come back into view (8)
27. The business of the occulist (5)
28. Flower for a yoga position (5)
29. Race around this area? (4)
30. Gives freedom about tenancies? (8)
31. Free from a duty (6)
32. Sailor on the road? (3)

Clues Down.

1. Such a climb is sometimes laborious (6)
2. Peeled off — clothing for example (8)
3. There's no future in such days (6)
4. So little — but it's superlative (7)
5. Prepare for something theatrical (8)
6. Pollen-bearing part of plant (6)
7. A big step to take (6)
15. Useless — whichever way you look at it (3)
16. Ma's turned into a boy! (3)
17. Radio — without cord (8)
19. This is useful for spelling things out (8)
20. Expression of dissent (7)
22. It's taken in a breath of fresh air (6)
23. It's accommodating for youthful walkers (6)
25. Reply and be responsible for (6)
26. A bit steep to be so curt (6)

153

Continued from page 152

"Alan! What on earth are *you* doing here?"

He'd come! Alan had actually come to see her, in the country, which he loathed.

"I could ask you the same question," he replied grimly. "Sitting on the floor kissing this . . . hippie!"

How old fashioned, she thought vaguely, and Charles got up. He was almost as tall as Alan, his jeans dusty and face very tanned beside Alan's city paleness.

"And who might you be?" Charles inquired politely.

"Kate's fiancé, that's who!" Alan replied.

Katie gasped. It was the first she'd heard of it. And suddenly, much as she longed for it, now the thought didn't seem quite so attractive.

Charles looked squarely at her then placed his half-full basket of tomatoes in her hands.

"I'll be charging overtime after all," he said, and left them, striding purposefully along the rows of nearly ripe tomatoes.

Alan stared at his rapidly-disappearing back.

"He works here? The hired help, and you were letting him kiss you? Katie, I'm surprised at you!"

Katie stuck out her chin. "I'm surprised, too, Alan. I didn't even know you and I were engaged!"

He looked embarrassed. "Well, to tell the truth, Kate, I missed you. I was going to propose to you in Torquay. Then you didn't come and — well, I suppose I can propose to you just as well in a greenhouse."

"No," she said abruptly. "No, Alan, don't. Because I'd have to say no and I don't want to hurt you." She heard the words come out before she even thought about it.

But they were true, she realised.

★   ★   ★   ★

The next day old Bob and his nephew turned up — but not Charles.

Perhaps, she thought, he's got more work to do in the office. However, Katie didn't have much time to think about it, for Babsie had come out in her spots and she rushed from one ailing child to the other.

Then a brief letter arrived.

Helping Hands Agency, it was headed. *I have terminated our contract. Please find bill enclosed.*
                                        Charles.

She stared at it, stunned. *He'd* terminated the contract! It was up to her, Kate, to give *him* notice! Goodness knows, he deserved it! Furiously she grabbed a pen and paper.

You have not terminated any contract. There wasn't one. I am giving you notice — for inefficiency. Therefore, I shall not pay your bill, which is exorbitant anyway.
                                        Kate.

THE next day he arrived, formally dressed as he had been the first day. A stranger. Charles again, not Charlie, who'd picked tomatoes with her all through a hot summer's afternoon.

Katie, who with two sick children was now more overworked than ever, felt a rush of sheer relief and pleasure at the sight of him. She wished she'd had time to change from jeans and brush out her hair.

But he didn't smile his usual gentle smile at her.

"What all this about inefficiency?" he demanded. She flushed.

"You — you didn't cook the bacon and eggs," she stammered.

He took an impulsive step towards her, then stopped.

"I thought your fiancé would take over. That's if he's even capable of breaking an egg, which I very much doubt," he added with a trace of bitterness.

"He's not my fiancé."

"Oh." He came closer. "Still overworked, are you?"

"Utterly." It all came out in a rush. "George has disappeared and Babsie's got measles and Uncle Henry sent me a postcard. He's staying *another* week!" she wailed.

"You know why, of course?"

She shook her head.

"He told me his housekeeper was on that package holiday. He wanted to make it up with her. He was going to ask her to marry him."

"He *was*?" It seemed that Charles had learned more about Uncle Henry in one day than she'd learned in two weeks, she thought with surprise.

Then Penelope came limping into the kitchen.

"Kate! Kate! George has just had kittens! In my wardrobe! What are you going to do?"

"Oh, no!" Katie cast a despairing cry heavenwards. "But he can't have!"

"Well, he has," Penelope said jubilantly. "Three of them!"

Kate looked at Charles. There was nothing else for it. "Would you? I mean, I don't know anything about cats!"

"You want to employ me again, then, Katie?" he asked seriously, and she nodded, her heart sinking. "Desperate enough to pay double overtime?"

She took a deep breath. If that was all he wanted, well all right. "If necessary."

"It's not," he said surprisingly. "Actually, I'm supposed to be on holiday. I'm just helping out my brother. He's the one who runs the Agency. I'm an architect, playing truant."

He held out his hand and she took it gladly.

"Come on," he said. "Let's go and find George. And you'd better find another name for him."

And they did.

They called him Henrietta — after Uncle Henry.

———— * **THE END** * ————

THERE was a cheerful greeting as the back door opened and a sailor walked in. On his shoulder was a monkey, wearing a red cloak and hat.

My mother was delighted to have this surprise visit from one of her sons during the last war, but the shock of seeing him and the passenger on his shoulder left her speechless. She just stared at the monkey with her mouth open — and the monkey did likewise.

My brother babbled the explanation: "The ship came in unex- pectedly for a refit; this is the ship's mascot, Jackie. I lived nearest to port so I'm responsible — couldn't leave him on board. It's all right, he's tame and used to people. And you'll like him. He's a character."

After tea my brother said casually, "Well, I must be going soon. I'll leave the monkey here."

''Leave it here?'' Mother screeched in alarm. "You can't do that."

"Well, it's only for a couple of days. I'll be home again then."

JACKIE
— Our Lovable Little
Mischief-Maker

He arrived out of the blue, says Nora Greenwood — Jackie, the cheeky little monkey who turned our home into his playground and our lives completely upside-down!

There followed half an hour of explanation, argument and instructions. Mother remained dubious.

"What about nights?" she asked with concern.

"No trouble," my brother soothed. "I'll make up a bed for him down here in this warm room and he'll sleep all night."

It was a nervous, tensed-up Mum who went to bed that night. She began to unwind and finally dropped off into an uneasy sleep. Suddenly, there was a "plop" on the bed and she was wide awake with fear. The monkey had arrived — for the night ! What my brother hadn't told Mother was that Jackie was used to sleeping with some-one, usually a sailor in a ham-mock.

The next morning, Mother, pale and tired, was outside the Post Office before nine o'clock waiting for the doors to open. As soon as the clerk was ready for business, she said tensely, "I want to send a telegram."

There was no hesitation about the wording on the form. She had planned it so many times in that suspense-filled night. She wrote quickly and deliberately:

"Come and get monkey. Mum."

My brother did come in response to that appealing wire — but he couldn't have Jackie back. My memory is hazy about the reason — it was something to do with the mysteries of wartime Naval decisions. At any rate, my brother didn't rejoin his ship and the monkey didn't rejoin my brother!

To be fair to my sailor brother, he smoothed the adoption process with aids like a huge cage for indoors and a chain and stake for outdoors, when weather permitted. To be honest, weather permitted more often in Mother's opinion than the monkey's!

WHEN Jackie was safe in his cage or secure on a lead, he was an amusing pet. His favourite possessions were a mirror, an old pair of spectacles and a hot water bottle. He was

By NORA GREENWOOD

fascinated by his reflection from any angle, preferably upside down, and derived almost as much pleasure from adjusting the mirror to catch the reflection of anybody else.

His antics with the specs produced smiles from the most stern-faced visitors. And he just loved a hot water bottle on a chilly night. He'd chatter and cuddle into it and if a hand approached it even in fun, he'd be on the defensive.

In the garden on his long lead, more freedom made Jackie more fun-loving. If our cat stretched out for a snooze in the sun, she had to judge her distance carefully. If she didn't she would get a rude awakening by the sharp pulling of her tail. And Jackie was always well out of reach before she'd realised what had happened.

The expression on the cat's face during those moments always made me feel sorry for her. She always seemed to be wondering what she'd done to deserve a monkey for a companion.

Our dog, Micky, and the monkey, however, had a good relationship, although I think Jackie had the better bargain of the friendship. You see, one of his favourite occupations was grooming, or "flea hunting" as we called it. So when he was tired of doing himself, he could do the dog. You will appreciate what a delightfully absorbing job that was when I tell you that Micky was an old-fashioned English sheepdog. And the dog seemed to enjoy the detailed cleansing operation.

One of our neighbours had a puppy who came and played with the monkey and it was an entertainment. About the same size, the pup tried hard to imitate the antics of the monkey and simply couldn't understand his own limitations.

Although the monkey cemented our friendship with that neighbour, he caused a rift in our relationship with another. On a summer morning when I was at home, I gave the monkey a bath in the garden, using a hair shampoo. As a nurse, I had bathed many a protesting patient but this was by far the most difficult challenge of my career.

Determined, damp and dishevelled, I completed the job. With a triumphant final flourish, I sprayed some of my perfume over the clean, fluffy, but still struggling monkey.

With a sudden leap, he went down the garden. I don't know whether it was the perfume that went to his head or whether it was sheer exuberance over feeling so clean. But that was the beginning of an action-packed day.

He started by jumping over the hedge. Then he climbed on to the neighbour's clothes line, pulled off most of the pegs and seemed to enjoy watching the wet washing fall to the ground.

We spent most of the day trying to lure him back to our patch of lawn but he was determined to enjoy the trees and the freedom of the garden. Needless to say, the cat disappeared!

The vicar called and we invited him into the garden because we wanted to keep an eye on the monkey. This was a mistake. In the middle of serious discussion, Jackie appeared from nowhere, leapt up the body of a seated vicar, snatched the spectacles off his nose and scampered away. The surprised and short-sighted cleric scrambled to his feet and groped a few aimless steps.

I left someone to console him and tried to follow the monkey. Jackie finally settled on top of the shed and spent a happy half hour or so peering through the specs from different positions. I can't remember how long it was before the specs were returned to their frustrated owner. But visits from the vicar were less frequent after that day!

A S Jackie grew older and bigger, his escapades increased. He used to escape from his stake in the garden in a Houdini-like manner. Then he escaped once too often.

Mother was making some pastry when Jackie entered the kitchen like a tornado. He sprang on to the pastry-strewn table and sent things flying, then with flour and dough-tipped feet he leapt on to everything, picking things up and dropping them as he went.

He lifted the lid off the kettle (fortunately cold) and stirred the water with a floury paw. Completing the circuit of the room, he landed on an unbaked treacle tart. At that act of sabotage, Mother emerged from her stunned state and sprang into action. She grabbed the nearest weapon — a broom.

A spectacular chase followed, from room to room, throughout the house. Now one loose monkey could do quite a lot of damage leaping around on its own. Put behind it one worried, frantic woman wielding a broom and you can imagine the fiasco.

Jackie and his treacly paws went up and down curtains and played along picture rails. He knocked down photos and ornaments and played an arpeggio on the opened piano. He went along the mantelpiece and with swipes of his tail demolished valuable vases that had miraculously survived our childhood.

Having completed the destruction downstairs, he bounded upstairs into a bedroom, followed by a breathless pursuer.

In one movement, he leapt on to the dressing-table, and whipped off the lid of a powder bowl. A quick swish with a paw into the lovely soft stuff scattered a perfumed dust storm. Then there was the inevitable crash of the glass lid before going on to the next stop. When a monkey takes off a lid, it never puts it back, just tosses it nonchalantly away!

Neatly evading Mother, he ran on with two more bedrooms to go — and spurred on by every missing swipe of the broom. Luckily for Jackie, in that last bedroom there was an open window and he escaped through it to the sound of the last crash.

Mother, shocked, shattered and defeated, fell on the nearest bed.

Later in the evening, slightly recovered with the help of brandy, she made arrangements for the immediate removal of Jackie. Among the monkey's juvenile admirers were two boys in the village, who had longed to own him. They were surprised and jubilant with the sudden and unexpected gift.

Later that year, we heard that Jackie had died, not of exhaustion as we expected, but from flu. And we were sad. He had really given us more laughs than trouble, and we shall always remember with affection the mascot monkey who did not rejoin his ship. ∎

"I WAS WRONG"

... and in one hasty moment, she condemned her daughter – and herself – to a lifetime of unhappiness.

MIRIAM KENT lay back in her deck-chair and gazed up at the sky. The sun, glancing through the leaves, made a bright, changing pattern in the garden around her, while the scent of the nearby lavender bush was strong in the still air. Lavender — the scent her mother had always worn . . .

She closed her eyes, and once again her loss stabbed deep inside her, a twisting, searing sorrow.

She tried to remember her mother's advice about moments like these.

Think of something beautiful, she had always said. When your spirits can't get any lower, think of something lovely.

When the sky is black, try to remember how it looked when it was blue. And when the trees are bare, think of the glory of summer . . .

Oh, Mother, she thought, it's not as easy as that.

The clouds have passed, the sky has turned blue, summer's here — but how can I see beauty in anything again? For you have gone now, for ever, leaving this aching weariness, these tears that never fall.

You and I were always close, Mother, she thought — even more so when Don died, leaving me with a baby to bring up.

Miriam shifted uneasily in her chair as she thought of her daughter, Julia. Remorse welled up inside her. Julia had come home that terrible day, needing comfort and understanding — deserving it.

And Miriam, her own heart leaden, just couldn't give any . . .

As Miriam had made her way back from the surgery that cold afternoon, the winter gloom had hung thickly around her. But the darkness inside her had been more real.

She should have guessed . . . prepared herself for this news. After all, her mother was in her 70s. But she had buried her anxiety deep inside her, refusing to face it.

Complete Story by PAMELA SPECK

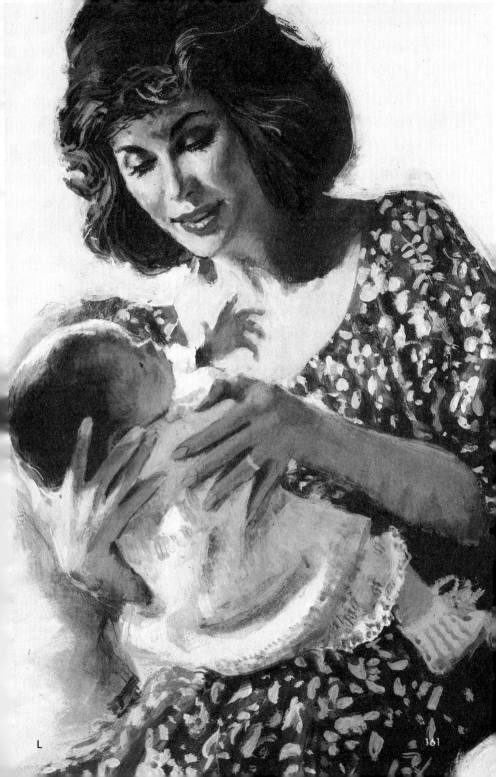

On the way into town, she'd told herself that Dr Blake was probably only concerned because her mother was becoming older and more frail. No doubt he was going to suggest it would be wiser if she went to live with Miriam.

But it hadn't been like that at all. When Miriam had come away from the surgery, she carried with her the shattering knowledge that her mother had less than six months to live . . .

Miriam found it impossible to imagine a world without her mother.

She had been there all through the golden years of childhood, there when Julia was born, and when Don had died.

Not living in the same house or even round the corner, but at the other end of town, retaining her own independence.

And gently she had made sure, in those first bleak months after Don's death, that Miriam had retained hers, too. But no matter how far away, she'd been there all the same. It had seemed as though she always would be . . .

THERE had been a radio playing when Miriam got back to the house. At first she'd thought she was imagining it. Julia was miles away at university.

Then a door had slammed above and there was the sound of footsteps on the stairs. Not light and quick like Julia's, but heavy, as hers had been all the way home.

"Julia? Julia, is that you?"

Julia had come down the stairs slowly, startling Miriam with her paleness, the shadows under her eyes.

Then Julia had spoken. "Mother, I'm pregnant."

The words had come out flatly, with no tone or life in them. Miriam's first thought had been — but that's not how it should be said. It should be sung, joyfully, clearly, so that everyone could hear and be happy for you. That was the way *she* had said it.

Only, she had been married with a home of her own. She had not been a student without a wedding ring . . .

From where she'd stood at the foot of the stairs, Miriam could only stare up at her daughter. Then the years had come back to her — years she would rather have forgotten.

She had spent them leaving her small daughter at nursery school and hurrying off to her job. While other people shared Julia's precious, unrepeatable young life, she had sat at an office desk, being a secretary, when she would rather have been a mother.

But it had been worthwhile in the end. When Julia got to university, it had seemed worth every moment of that long, long labour of love. But just then, it had seemed it had all been for nothing . . .

She hadn't even known she was speaking. Then she'd noticed Julia's face grow paler, had heard her say again and again, "I'm sorry, I'm *sorry*."

Only then had she realised she'd been recalling those years out loud. As if in some sort of nightmare she couldn't wake from, she'd heard a woman's voice shrilling on and on. Dimly, she'd been aware that it was her own.

Somewhere inside her, she'd heard another voice saying, *Stop! You shouldn't be behaving like this, you should be helping her. Giving her all the support and sympathy she needs right now — just as you need it, too.*

But she hadn't been able to stop, not until she'd seen her daughter's fac crumple, seen her turn and flee up the stairs. Only then had her torrent of words halted.

If only it hadn't happened then, with the doctor's words hammering in her brain. For one awful moment her sanity had seemed to desert her completely.

Miriam had pictured this situation before. She'd thought most parents with daughters did. But in her imagination she had behaved very differently.

She had seen herself as a pillar of strength, a fount of understanding, a mother in every sense of the word. But faced with reality, she had failed her child.

She had got up to put the kettle on, meaning to make them both a cup of tea. She'd planned to call Julia down so they could sit together and discuss everything rationally.

She'd apologise and tell Julia about Mother. This was something they had to face together. Her mother's last days must be filled with love and comfort.

But at that point the front door had slammed. Julia's footsteps had been clear and distinct, and they hadn't been heavy this time.

Miriam, watching from the window, had been speechless, helpless, as her daughter hailed a passing taxi and vanished down the road.

She'd wanted to cry, "Come back! I didn't mean a word of it, you must know that!"

But again, as if in a nightmare, no words came . . .

NOW in her deck-chair, under the tree, her mother's words came back to her again.

Think of something beautiful. Not of those long months spent nursing a failing mother. Not of the sleepless nights, wondering where her daughter was, what she could possibly be doing.

No, don't think of any of those things, Miriam told herself. Think of Mother as she was when she was alive, those days when she came to visit. Summer days like this one, when you sat like this in the garden, waiting for her.

Three short peals of the doorbell would announce her, and she'd let herself in with her own key. Even before you saw her, the scent of lavender would tell you she was there.

Miriam settled the cushion more comfortably under her head. The warm day had made her drowsy, and her eyelids closed. Her mind drifted aimlessly, half-conscious of the birdsong, the passing of an occasional car, a dog barking in the distance.

It was as if she were dreaming. She heard a sound she'd thought she would never hear again — three short, sharp peals of the doorbell . . .

She sat bolt upright. She *must* have been dreaming.

But, just the same, something made her rise. She went into the house. There, all was quiet and still. Yet the sound of the chimes seemed to hang in the air, as if the bell really had rung.

In the hall, she stood stock-still, for there was something else lingering in the air. A light, haunting fragrance she had known and loved since childhood — lavender . . .

FOR one brief moment, she thought she had dreamed it all. These past months had all been just a nightmare.

But the moment passed and reality returned. And with reality came something else — a memory, a memory of a little girl who had always sniffed appreciatively when her grandmother was near, and said:

"Oh, Granny, you do smell nice!"

She turned swiftly, hope rising high inside her.

"Julia?" she called. "Julia — darling, is that you?"

There was no reply. But as she held her breath, the living-room door opened slowly, and her daughter stood there.

"Oh, Mother." Her eyes filled. "I went to Gran's first . . ."

Miriam held out her arms.

"It was my fault," Miriam murmured. "I said things I shouldn't have, things I didn't mean. I must have been out of my mind."

Then she remembered why Julia had left home. Oh, please don't have parted with the child, she prayed, as she held her daughter close. I know everything started off wrong, but let's make it right now!

Then she saw him standing at the door — a tall, young man.

"Mum," Julia said happily. "This is David. We got married a while ago. And here . . ."

She went into the living-room. "Here's someone we thought you'd like to meet!"

Miriam's heart sang at the sight of the bundle in her daughter's arms. Gently she took the baby from her and peered into the tiny face.

The song in her heart grew so loud, it seemed impossible that the others could not hear it. Familiar features lay before her, familiar eyes looked back into her own.

"Doesn't she look like Gran?" Julia said proudly.

Miriam nodded. "Oh, yes. She's her grandmother's girl, all right."

She held the baby close, putting her cheek gently against the fresh, pink one.

Think of something beautiful, her mother had said. But at that moment she knew that if she had tried for the rest of her life, she could never have thought of anything as beautiful as this.

———————— * **THE END** * ————————

It was a time
for memories —
on this special
day when his
daughter was
leaving to begin
a new life.

Memories
Of
Linda

**Complete Story by
SARAH BURKHILL**

NEIL MARTIN took a deep breath, and with some difficulty
succeeded in buttoning the jacket of his dress suit.

He was getting fat.

Well, not fat exactly, Neil amended, surveying himself in the living-room mirror, more sort of — what was the word he was looking for? Well built? Perhaps cuddly?

Neil frowned. Fat. That was the word. The monkey suit he'd worn when he married Janet 23 years ago had been a size 38. Now he had expanded to a 42. Indisputable proof?

Turning away from the mirror, Neil began pacing up and down the floor. What was keeping everyone? Did no-one else realise there was a wedding in half an hour?

He stubbed out his cigarette and immediately lit another. The last time he had smoked like that was at his daughter's birth. Now here he was, 22 years and four stone later, waiting to lead her down the aisle.

He closed his eyes and those 22 years unfolded before him. Suddenly he was back in the hospital pacing the floor . . .

HE broke out in a cold sweat that had nothing to do with the hospital's over-efficient heating system. And as his gaze caught Janet's young brother, Harry, there as moral support, he thought back over all the objections that had occupied him in the preceding nine months. He remembered that his reaction to prospective fatherhood hadn't been one of total delight.

It wasn't that he had anything against children — well, other people's children, at any rate.

You didn't have to get up in the middle of the night for other people's children, or change their nappies, or feed them, or . . .

Suddenly he rounded on Harry.

"What if I don't like it once it's here?" he asked, trembling with this new and horrifying prospect.

His brother-in-law shrugged. "I don't know much about it, not having any, but isn't everyone supposed to like their offspring? I think it's something that comes with prams and cots and other such things."

Neil shook his head gravely. "Not necessarily. Oh, I expect I shall *love* it. That's different. But I might not actually *like* it."

He descended further into his gloom. "Can you imagine having to live for years and years with something you didn't even like? It would be worse than —"

He broke off as a nurse came in.

"Mr Martin?" Her smile faded slightly at the collection of cigarette ends that littered the floor, and she glanced pointedly at the *No Smoking* sign before going on:

"You've got a baby daughter. Seven pounds two ounces. Both are doing fine."

"Both!" Neil said in horror. "You don't mean there's —"

"Shut up, you idiot. She means Janet," Harry whispered, smiling apologetically at the nurse.

"Well, go on." He dug an elbow into Neil's side. "Don't you want to see them?"

At the bedside, Neil ran a finger down his wife's cheek and kissed

"AND I QUOTE . . ."

Brian Johnston (1912-), British radio and TV commentator, educated Eton and Oxford, was one of the earliest BBC cricket commentators and has continued to act in this capacity. He also successfully presented the radio programme *Down Your Way* for many years.

I asked the old lady whether she had received a telegram from the Queen on her hundredth birthday. "Oh yes," she said, "I did, but I was very disappointed. It wasn't in her own handwriting."

---

her softly. He was faintly surprised to find the old tales about radiant motherhood were true after all — at least in this case. Janet had never looked lovelier.

"Never mind about me," she said when he'd told her so. "What about your daughter? Isn't she gorgeous?"

Janet nodded towards the cot at her bedside, and a little reluctantly Neil peered inside.

"Beautiful," he said. "Just like her old mum!"

Actually, the only thing he could think of which bore the slightest resemblance to the wrinkled bundle was a large, scarlet-painted prune, but that didn't seem the best of comparisons to make.

"What are we going to call her?" Janet went on. "We haven't really given much thought to names."

She considered the matter for a moment, then said, "What about Emma? I rather like that."

Neil made a face and frowned at the baby in the cot. It didn't look like an Emma — but then again, it didn't really look like anything he'd ever seen.

"I'll bring a book of names when I come tonight," he promised.

JANET and baby Martin had been home for only two hours when the relatives descended.

"She's exactly like your grandma in the photographs of her as a baby," Janet's mother informed her. "I wish she had lived to see this day. She'd have been as proud as a peacock!"

Neil's mother, who was secretly convinced the new baby was the image of her late husband, George, hastily changed the subject.

"What are you going to call here? Have you decided on a name yet?"

"I was thinking about Emma," Janet began hesitantly, "only Neil doesn't seem to fancy that much."

Grandma Gordon raised an eyebrow at her daughter.

"But we've never had any Emmas in the family. What do you want to go calling her that for?"

She shook her head and dismissed the proposed name. "Now, what about Beatrice, after your grandmother? There's a lovely name for you, and it means 'giving happiness.' I think that would be most suitable. *Most* suitable."

Neil was about to suggest — tactfully — that if she was so enamoured of the name Beatrice she should have bestowed it on one of her own brood, but he didn't get the chance.

Neil's mother sniffed huffily.

"I really would have thought Georgina the most obvious choice — for your father," she said to Neil. "You know how pleased he would have been to have a grandchild called after him."

Neil retired to the corner where Emma/Georgina/Beatrice lay

○ The ship is sinking. We must try and save it. Help me get it into the lifeboat.

○ Listen. Someone's screaming in agony. Fortunately I speak it fluently.

○ Are you going to come quietly or do I have to use ear-plugs?

○ Sit down and warm yourself by the candle.

◄ Spike holding forth in recent years.

gurgling in her cot, blissfully unaware of the momentous decision that was being made.

Next day Janet put the phone down and sighed.

"Well, that's the fourth suggestion in," she informed him.

The grandmas were due back in again at any moment, and Neil was on the point of making his escape to the local. With a bit of luck, Harry would be there.

"Aunt Hilda heard we were stuck for a name," Janet went on, "and she phoned to suggest Miranda."

"Who's that after?" Neil asked suspiciously.

"Nobody," Janet replied. "She just likes it!"

He raised his eyes to the ceiling. "Miranda Martin! Sounds like a variety of rose!"

Neil related the latest development to Harry, who was in the process of finishing a half pint of lager with remarkable haste.

"Pity you hadn't had a monkey," he said, laying the glass down on the bartop. "You could just have called it Jacko and been done with it!"

Neil surveyed him gloomily. "It's all very well for you to laugh. Just wait till it's your turn!"

"Give me a chance, I'm not even married yet." Harry looked at his watch. "Hey, sorry to leave you, squire, but I've got to go."

He winked. "Meeting this smashing new bird from the office. Linda Dalziel. Absolute dream! See you."

Neil stared into his almost-full glass. Linda! That was it, a nice, pert, no-nonsense name.

He abandoned his beer and set off determinedly for the field of battle. After all, it was his daughter, too!

"Linda!"

Both grandmas, Aunt Hilda, and Janet looked at him doubtfully.

"It's an old German name, meaning a serpent," Grandma Gorden read disapprovingly from the book of names. "I'm not having a granddaughter named after a snake!"

"Nonsense." Neil brushed aside all objections. "Snakes were worshipped in old Germany. Goddesses, that's what they were."

"That's all very well, Neil," Janet said. "But we happen to be living in twentieth-century Britain!"

He was not to be put off. "OK, then. In Spanish, Linda means beautiful. What could be more appropriate?"

He lifted his daughter from the cot and looked at her. It was remarkable, but she *was* beautiful. Gone was the wrinkled prune look, and in its place was a tiny, lovely, perfect little girl.

"I don't actually dislike Linda, but I still want her to be called Emma," Janet said firmly.

"Beatrice!"

"Georgina!"

"Miranda!"

Neil ran his fingers through his hair.

"Well, there's only one thing for it, then," he said decisively.

CROSSWORD

SOLUTION TO CROSSWORD ON PAGE 153.

ACROSS — 3 Bit, 8 Spotty, 9 Identity, 10 Gigi, 11 Olive, 12 Main, 13 Slippers, 14 Rented, 16 Shadows, 18 Related, 21 Mother, 24 Reappear, 27 Eyes, 28 Lotus, 29 Acre, 30 Releases, 31 Exempt, 32 Tar.

DOWN — 1 Uphill, 2 Stripped, 3 Bygone, 4 Tiniest, 5 Rehearse, 6 Stamen, 7 Stride, 15 Dud, 16 Sam, 17 Wireless, 19 Alphabet, 20 Protest, 22 Oxygen, 23 Hostel, 25 Answer, 26 Abrupt.

"We'll have to put all the names in a hat and draw one out."

Obligingly, Grandma Martin took off her hat, and Neil carefully wrote a name on each of five sheets of paper.

He was about to extract one when the telephone shrilled and he frowned.

"If that's Harry putting Jacko up for serious consideration, tell him he's too late. Or on second thoughts, I'll tell him myself!"

He returned a few moments later. "It was Aunt Jane, wanting to know if we'd decided yet. She's got a christening mug she wants to get inscribed, so I told her to hang on and I'd let her know in a minute."

Neil offered the hat to Janet, and gingerly she drew out a piece of paper. Suddenly everyone fell still while Janet unfolded the paper.

"It's Linda," she said.

NEIL stubbed out his cigarette and went back to the mirror. It didn't seem like 22 years since Linda Martin first saw the light of day, he thought.

Soon she would be getting another name bestowed on her — Mrs Philip Read.

"That's if we ever get to the church at all, the time they're taking," he said out loud.

"Don't panic," Janet told him as she came into the room. "Another five minutes and she'll be ready. There's plenty of time."

Neil looked at his wife. "You know, you don't seem half old enough to be the mother of the bride. You've hardly changed at all since Linda was born."

He shifted uncomfortably, then went on, "Actually, I've just been thinking about that. I've got a confession to make."

He paused. "Do you remember . . . All the names I was supposed to put in that hat . . . You know, when we couldn't decide on one? Well, I wrote Linda on all the papers."

Janet smiled. "I know. You don't think I'd have trusted you over something like that, do you? When you went out to answer the phone, I changed them round again. I put in the correct ones."

Neil stared at her. "You mean I won fair and square, and I've been feeling guilty all these years for nothing?"

He broke off as the door opened, and looked at his daughter. It would have been difficult to recognise his baby in the bride that stood before him now, and Neil swallowed hard.

"Well, I wouldn't say it was for nothing," Janet said, as the bridesmaids came in and gathered round their sister.

Emma, Miranda, Trixie and Georgina gave her a questioning look. "What wasn't for nothing?"

Neil's eyes misted as he surveyed his five daughters, and he blinked several times.

"Never you mind," he said sternly. "Never you mind."

——————— * **THE END** * ———————

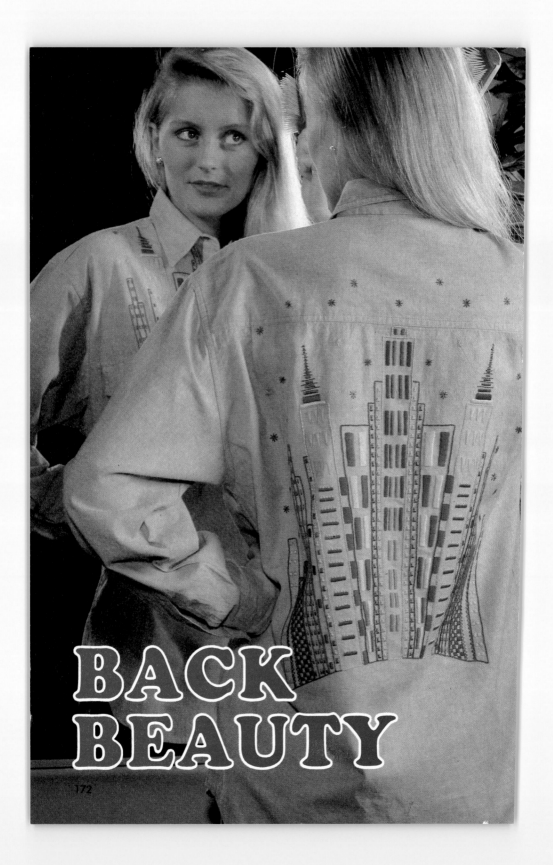

BACK BEAUTY

If you'd like a plain shirt to look interesting, just follow our instructions to give your back view a new image!

Materials Required – Anchor Stranded Cotton: 4 skeins each Rose Madder 59, Antique Gold 306; 3 skeins each Violet 101, Jade 189; 2 skeins each Peacock Blue 167, 170 and 1 skein Delphinium 123.

Use 6 strands for Straight Stitch in 189 on buildings, 4 strands for Sheaf Stitch and 3 strands for rest of embroidery.

Denim shirt similar to illustration.

Dressmaker's carbon paper.

Milward International Range crewel needles No. 7 for 3 strands, No. 6 for 4 strands and No. 5 for 6 strands.

The combined grid diagram and diagram 1 gives half of the design, centre indicated by large broken lines. The grid markings round the edge of the design represent 2.5 cm. Join up the grid lines vertically and horizontally using a coloured pencil. Scale up the design as given on to large piece of paper. Mark the centre back of shirt lengthwise with a line of basting stitches. The basting stitches should coincide with the large broken lines on grid diagram. With back of shirt facing and using dressmaker's carbon paper, trace the outlines of the scaled-up design (omitting arrows and numbers) on to right half of back, positioning as desired. To complete design, trace in reverse on to left half. Parts of the roof tops may be traced to the front yoke if desired. Work embroidery following diagram 1 and key to diagram. All parts similar to numbered parts are worked in the same colour and stitch. On completion of embroidery press on the wrong side.

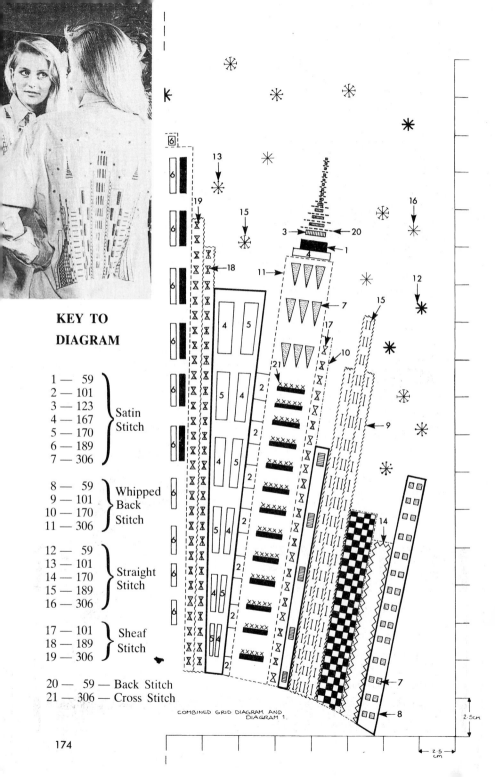

KEY TO DIAGRAM

1 — 59
2 — 101
3 — 123
4 — 167 } Satin Stitch
5 — 170
6 — 189
7 — 306

8 — 59
9 — 101 } Whipped Back Stitch
10 — 170
11 — 306

12 — 59
13 — 101
14 — 170 } Straight Stitch
15 — 189
16 — 306

17 — 101
18 — 189 } Sheaf Stitch
19 — 306

20 — 59 — Back Stitch
21 — 306 — Cross Stitch

COMBINED GRID DIAGRAM AND
DIAGRAM 1.